The Feast of Christmas

The Feast of Christmas

Joseph F. Kelly

LITURGICAL PRESS
Collegeville, Minnesota

www.litpress.org

Nihil Obstat: Reverend Robert Harren, *Censor deputatus*
Imprimatur: ✠Most Reverend John F. Kinney, J.C.D., D.D., Bishop
of Saint Cloud, Minnesota, May 7, 2010.

Cover design by David Manahan, OSB. *The Flight into Egypt*,
Fra Angelico, Florence, Italy, 1450.

Scripture texts in this work are taken from the *New Revised Standard Version Bible: Catholic Edition* © 1989, 1993, Division of Christian Education of the National Council of the Churches of Christ in the United States of America. Used by permission. All rights reserved.

1   2   3   4   5   6   7   8   9

Library of Congress Cataloging-in-Publication Data

Kelly, Joseph F. (Joseph Francis), 1945–
    The feast of Christmas / Joseph F. Kelly.
        p. cm.
    Includes bibliographical references.
    ISBN 978-0-8146-3325-0 — ISBN 978-0-8146-3932-0 (e-book)
    1. Christmas.   I. Title.

BV45.K435   2010
263'.91509—dc22   2010017075

*To Margaret and David Mason,
and to the memory of Richard Clancey*

Contents

Preface

This brief book surveys how Christmas was celebrated religiously over the centuries. It differs from most general studies, which focus on the religious Christmas until the end of the Middle Ages but then turn to the rise of the secular one. As I make clear in the book, I value both the religious and secular Christmas and see no inherent opposition between the two. My purpose here is simply to highlight the religious one, not least because I know of no other book that has done this. Most histories of Christmas focus on the last 250 years when the familiar celebration with trees, lights, and Santa became popular.

This book has the advantage of a survey, showing individual episodes and events against a larger background. It also has the disadvantage of a survey, a cursory treatment of topics and the omission of many more. A detailed, full-fledged history of the religious Christmas would be multivolume and thus unsuitable for the general reader for whom this book is intended.

The book covers the whole history of the feast, but from the late Middle Ages until today, it focuses on what happened in Great Britain and the United States. I do not mean to play down the many important contributions of other societies, but this book is written for English-speaking readers, and so it concentrates on those countries.

At John Carroll University I teach a course on the history of Christmas. Over the years my students have asked me many good questions that have sharpened not only my understanding of the subject but also of the kinds of topics that would interest the general reader. If you find this book helpful, my students can take much of the credit. Any deficiencies in the book are the sole property of the author.

My thanks to Peter Dwyer, director of Liturgical Press, and Hans Christoffersen, editorial director, for their interest and support. Thanks also to Mary Stommes, who supervised the editing. My graduate assistant Bridget Ludwa read most of this book, and I am grateful for her help. As always, my sincerest thanks go to my wife Ellen, a loving and generous spouse, who took time from her own busy schedule and made myriad sacrifices so that I would have time to write.

This book is dedicated to my good, longtime friends, Margaret and David Mason, and to the memory of Richard Clancey, a wonderful, much-loved, and still-missed friend to the Masons, my wife, and me.

CHAPTER ONE

Christianity without Christmas

At first glance, this chapter seems to have the wrong title. Christianity has always had Christmas. Actually, no. Although we commonly call the birth of Jesus "the First Christmas," it was not. Christmas is the feast in honor of Christ's birth; the birth itself is rightly called the Nativity. No first-century evidence survives for any kind of feast in honor of Jesus' birth; in fact, not much evidence of the birth survives.

The Christian New Testament consists of twenty-seven books, twenty-one of which are classified as epistles or letters. The book of Revelation contains visions of the imminent end of the age, while the Acts of the Apostles recounts the early history of the Christian community with a strong focus on the career of the apostle Paul. These twenty-three books contain occasional references to Jesus' earthly life, but only the four gospels of Matthew, Mark, Luke, and John recount anything biographical about Jesus, and only two of them, Matthew and Luke, tell of Jesus' birth. The conclusion is inescapable. No matter how much we value Christmas and its traditions today, the earliest Christians had very little interest in Jesus' birth.

Why?

No early Christian writer actually wrote, "We are not interested in Jesus' birth because . . . ," but scholars think they can pinpoint the reason. Ample evidence in the New Testament books, especially Paul's epistles, makes it clear that the

1

Christians anticipated a very early end to the world. They literally thought that it could happen tomorrow. With no future, they apparently had little interest in the past. But nothing wears down apocalyptic expectation like passing time, and in an era when most people failed to reach the age of forty, many Christians inevitably wondered why so many had died and the end had still not come. As the end receded into the future, Christians looked to their past. Around the year 70, a Christian named Mark wrote a gospel, a theologized account of Jesus' public career. Significantly, it included no mention of his birth.

Mark's innovation caught on, and other writers followed him. Next to do so were Matthew and Luke. Both knew Mark's gospel and generally followed his outline. They wrote in the eighties of the first century, and both included a Nativity narrative. Since Mark's gospel proved that a gospel did not necessarily have to have an infancy narrative, what prompted Matthew and Luke to include one?

The two evangelists never said explicitly why they did so, but biblical scholars believe the cause was Mark's account of Jesus' baptism by John the Baptist. In that gospel God recognizes Jesus as his son as he emerges from the Jordan River after his baptism by John. Like all early Christians, Mark believed John to be a forerunner of Jesus, but not all of John's disciples did. In his book the Acts of the Apostles Luke tells how disciples of John continued his movement after his death, and not just in the Holy Land but in other parts of the Roman Empire, such as Egypt and Asia Minor (modern Turkey). A third-century text from Roman Syria says that John, not Jesus, was the Christ, that is, the Messiah.

Although John's movement never achieved great influence, Matthew and Luke feared that Mark's account might imply that God did not recognize Jesus as his son until John's baptism. Even worse, some believers might see a causal relationship between the baptism and the divine recognition. Therefore, the two evangelists set out to make it clear that

God had recognized Jesus as his son right from his conception, and they did so by adding the infancy narratives to their accounts of Jesus' public ministry, death, and resurrection. The infancy narratives occupy the first two chapters of both gospels. When modern believers read these accounts (the magi, the shepherds, the star), we do so in the wonderful context of Christmas. The accounts appear familiar and even heartwarming. But there was no Christmas in the first century, and the two evangelists did not write their accounts for a nonexistent feast. They wrote those chapters as introductions to their entire gospels, and to understand the infancy narratives we must understand their role in those gospels.

As we shall see, the two evangelists did not agree on all points, but they clearly drew from some common sources. Both agree that Jesus was born in Bethlehem during the reign of Herod the Great, the Roman-appointed king who ruled Judea from 37 to 4 B.C. Both identify his parents as Joseph and Miriam (Mary in English) and say that, after his birth, the family lived in Nazareth. Both evangelists point to a sign in the sky, although Matthew says it was a star and Luke that it was an angel. Both concur that visitors came to see the Holy Family, although Matthew says they were magi and Luke that they were shepherds. Both agree that the birth of Jesus fulfilled prophecies of the Old Testament and that Mary conceived virginally.

Where did Matthew and Luke get this information? Older generations of Christians thought it came from Mary, especially the material in Luke, who says much about her, but that was when scholars thought the gospels were written much sooner than the eighties of the first century, when Mary would have been more than a century old, almost impossible for that era. Scholars now believe that accounts of Jesus' birth, some of which could have originated with Mary, became part of the general collection of traditions about Jesus that started to circulate shortly after his death and resurrection.

The Gospel of Matthew

In the centuries before Jesus' birth, many Jews left the Holy Land and migrated to some of the Eastern Mediterranean cities, such as Antioch in Syria and Alexandria in Egypt. The presence of Jews outside the Holy Land is called the Diaspora, the Greek word for "dispersion." Living in these largely Gentile areas, the Jews came to speak Greek and even produced a Greek translation of the Old Testament. Matthew was a Diasporan Jew, a native Greek speaker, who may have lived in Judea for a while since his gospel reflects a knowledge of local customs.

We know little about him. Tradition identified him as the Matthew who was one of Jesus' twelve apostles, but modern scholars disproved that some time ago. Matthew the evangelist clearly relied upon Mark's gospel, but Mark was not one of the twelve apostles. This means that if the evangelist were one of the apostles, then someone who was an eyewitness to Jesus' public career would be getting information and modeling his gospel on information provided by someone who was not an eyewitness. This and other matters, mostly literary, make it clear that the author of the first gospel was not one of the twelve apostles. All we can say about Matthew was that he was a Diasporan Jew, probably from Roman Syria, who had an excellent education, since his gospel, a theological masterpiece, reflects considerable learning.

Readers of Matthew's gospel quickly notice his emphasis on Jesus' fulfillment of Old Testament prophecies; his infancy narrative alone includes five of them. Matthew also had a familiarity with Jewish laws and customs, and he portrays Jesus as a good Jew, obedient to the law. Clearly the evangelist needed to emphasize Jesus' Jewishness to his readers, which means that many of his readers were Diasporan Jews who had converted to Christianity but who understandably worried about the relation between their new faith and their former one. Matthew recognized those concerns, so throughout his gospel he emphasizes Jesus' Jewishness, although he makes it clear that the Christian message went to all people.

This gospel opens with a genealogy that traces Jesus' descent from Abraham, father of the Jewish people, through the great king David, down to Joseph and Mary, a standard Old Testament approach his readers would have recognized. Matthew tells us that Joseph and Mary were not living together when she was found to be pregnant, yet he refers to Joseph as her husband (1:19). In ancient Judea, when a couple announced their engagement, they were considered husband and wife even though they would usually live with their parents for a while after the engagement (people usually got married in their teens in those days). Joseph believed his wife had committed adultery, but an angel of the Lord appeared to him in a dream to tell him that Mary was pregnant by the Holy Spirit and was guiltless of any wrongdoing. Thanks to endless artistic portrayals of the angel Gabriel's annunciation of Jesus' birth to Mary, most Christians think of that alone as "the annunciation." But here Matthew reports that an unnamed angel made the announcement to Joseph. Interestingly, Matthew does not say where Mary and Joseph lived.

The angel spoke to Joseph in a dream. People in the ancient world, including the Jews, believed that deities would speak to them via dreams. The angel also told Joseph that Jesus' virginal conception fulfills the prophecy of Isaiah that a virgin would conceive and bring forth a son who would be called Emmanuel (Hebrew for "God with us"), something his converted Jewish readers would surely have appreciated.

Matthew next recounts how Jesus was born in Bethlehem during the reign of Herod, the Roman-appointed, half-Jewish tyrant. Suddenly "magi from the East" appear in the story. We all know who they were: three kings named Melchior, Caspar, and Balthasar, who rode on camels to see the newborn king. Alas, no. Matthew simply says "magi." The familiar "three kings" would emerge in Christian tradition in the following centuries.

The word "magi" usually meant Persian astrologers, and these magi followed a new star to Judea. Believing the star heralded the birth of a king, they went to the court of the reigning king, who became frightened at the thought of an infant rival. Herod's court scholars told him that the child promised in the prophecies would be born in Bethlehem, so Herod sent the magi there under the condition that they would report back to him. They went to Bethlehem, offered the Holy Family their gifts, and then, being warned in a dream (that is, receiving a sign from God), returned to their home a different way.

The infuriated Herod, who could not find the actual child, tried to eliminate the threat by killing all the infant boys in Bethlehem up to the age of two. Warned in a dream, the Holy Family escaped to Egypt, while Herod's soldiers killed the other children, known in Christian tradition as the Holy Innocents. Matthew finishes his account of Jesus' birth with two more dreams. In the first an angel told Joseph that Herod was dead and that he could return home. As Joseph prepared for the return, he learned that Herod's son Archelaus had succeeded to the throne, and he feared what the new king might do. An angel appeared to him in another dream and told him to go to Galilee and to settle in a town called Nazareth, which would fulfill a prophecy and explain why Jesus grew up in Nazareth.

As gospel introductions, the infancy narratives contain theology as well as history. Matthew makes comparisons between Moses and Jesus, both of whose lives were in danger when they were infants. The evangelist's converted Jewish readers would know and appreciate that. Furthermore, Matthew shows that when Jesus was born, the Jewish rulers (but not the people) sought his death but the pagan Gentile magi venerated him. At the time of Jesus' death, when the Jewish rulers (but, again, not the people) sought his death, another pagan Gentile, the wife of Pontius Pilate, spoke up on his behalf. When we recall that the four gospels dealt primarily with Jesus' public ministry and death, we can see how Matthew relates the birth and death accounts.

The Gospel of Luke

Contemporary with Matthew's gospel, that of Luke targeted a different audience. Luke was a Gentile from the Eastern Mediterranean, and he emphasized that Jesus came to save all people. Whereas Matthew's genealogy traces Jesus' lineage back to Abraham, father of the Jewish people, Luke's genealogy, which is not in his infancy narrative, goes back to Adam, the father of all people. Luke also wrote a second book, the Acts of the Apostles, which, focusing on the apostle Paul, recounts the early Christians' acceptance of the Gentiles into the church and the geographical movement of the faith from Judea into Asia Minor, Greece, and then Rome.

But Luke embraced more than ethnic and geographical universalism; he also focused on social universalism. His gospel emphasizes Jesus' concern for the poor and downtrodden, for those who suffer, and, very significantly for the ancient world, for women. Luke's accent on women appears most clearly in his infancy account where he focuses on Elizabeth, mother of John the Baptist, and Mary, the mother of Jesus. In fact, most of the biblical passages that Christians associate with Mary— the annunciation, the visitation, the *Magnificat*, the trip to Bethlehem, the presentation of the infant in the Temple, and the trip to Jerusalem when Jesus was twelve—all appear in the first two chapters of Luke's gospel.

Luke opens his gospel with a dedication to a nobleman named Theophilus, his literary patron who subsidized his work. He then moves to the announcement by the angel Gabriel to the priest Zachary that he and his wife Elizabeth, who are both elderly, will have a son whom they will name John. Matthew does not mention John the Baptist in his infancy narrative, but Luke deals with him directly, emphasizing that the child of Elizabeth and Zachary will be a great man but that he will prepare the way for a greater one. This would nullify any misinterpretation of Mark's account of Jesus' baptism by John.

The gospel then recounts Gabriel's annunciation of the birth of Jesus to the Virgin Mary, who lives in Nazareth of

Galilee. Here we see a discrepancy between Matthew's and Luke's accounts because Luke says Mary originally lived in Nazareth, while Matthew says the Holy Family went there from Egypt because they were afraid to return to Judea. The accounts cannot be reconciled. Both evangelists knew that Jesus' parents lived in Nazareth, but apparently they did not know for sure how they came to be there.

The angel informs Mary that the "Holy Spirit will come upon you, and the power of the Most High will overshadow you," assuring her that her pregnancy is part of God's plan (Luke 1:35). Gabriel also makes predictions about the future of her son, whom she is to name Jesus.

After this, Mary visits the elderly and pregnant Elizabeth, who addresses her as "the mother of my Lord," another emphasis by Luke that John the Baptist does not equal Jesus since "Lord" is a word for the divine. Mary responds with a poem later called the *Magnificat* because in the Middle Ages, when educated people spoke Latin, the first words of this poem were *Magnificat anima mea*, which means "My soul magnifies (the Lord)." The first word came to stand for the poem. When Mary returns home three months later, Elizabeth gives birth to John, and his father Zachary makes yet another prediction about him, again stressing his role as a forerunner of someone greater. Luke has effectively made it clear that Jesus' baptism by John had no role in God's recognition of Jesus as his son.

Now Luke turns to the birth of Jesus with some of the gospel's most famous words: "In those days a decree went out from Caesar Augustus that all the world [Roman Empire] should be registered" (2:1). Joseph and Mary travel from Nazareth to Bethlehem to register, but they must stay in a stable because they could find no room in an inn. (Luke just says that there was no room, never even hinting about a rude or cruel innkeeper, a villainous staple of later traditions.) The evangelist does not mention a star, but he does speak of a sign in the sky, in this case an angelic apparition to some shepherds. Significantly, Luke focuses on what the birth of Jesus will do for poor people, here represented by the shepherds.

Since many Gentiles had reservations about the much-maligned Christians, Luke shows how Jesus' parents obeyed not only the Roman law by registering for the census but also Jewish law by having their son circumcised. Although Luke does not focus on prophecies as Matthew does, he recounts how the Holy Family encountered two prophets in the Temple in Jerusalem, Simeon and Anna, who both prophesy how Jesus would redeem his people, that is, both Jews and Gentiles.

Luke closes his infancy narrative with the only account of Jesus' life between his birth and public career: his parents' taking him to the Temple, leaving without him, and then finding him there, safe and sound, three days later. Although an integral part of Luke's infancy narrative, this episode never became part of the Christmas story.

Theologically, Matthew and Luke succeeded brilliantly because their fellow Christians accepted that God's recognition of Jesus as his son by the river Jordan had nothing causal to do with Jesus' baptism by John. Inadvertently the two evangelists had also created the basis for one of Christianity's greatest feasts.

After the New Testament

No New Testament book written after these two gospels mentions Jesus' birth, and, in the first century, it appeared the infancy narratives would play no role in Christianity. But two forces changed that.

By the middle of the second century, as the Christian population became increasingly Gentile, the Christians concluded that the Bible should include not only the inspired books of the Old Testament but also books written by Christians. But which ones? The Christians debated that until the mid-fourth century when they settled on the twenty-seven books now in the New Testament. Yet as soon as they began to compile their own list of inspired books, or *canon*, in the early second century, they included the four gospels that modern Christians know so well. This meant that Matthew and Luke's infancy narratives would be part of the Christian Bible, and they would never be lost or forgotten, and no Christian could or would ignore them.

The second development was rethinking the Christians' belief that at any moment but definitely before any believers died, Jesus would return to earth and the end of the age would occur. This widespread belief effectively removed the Christians from history since at any moment they would be entering an eternal world. But by the early second century, when Jesus had been dead for many decades, fewer and fewer Christians believed in an imminent end but instead followed the evangelist Luke, who, in his book the Acts of the Apostles, insisted that the Holy Spirit will work in the Christian community until Jesus returns (although he probably did not think that the church would go on for two millennia more). The second-century Christians realized that they too would be part of the world's history, and this prompted an interest in their own history. They paid more attention to the gospels, including the infancy narratives, and we have some rather strange proof for that: they began composing their own gospels.

Expanding the Infancy Narratives

When modern Christians think of "the gospels," they naturally think of Matthew, Mark, Luke, and John. But there were actually dozens of gospels written in the first centuries of Christian history; there were also other epistles, acts, and even apocalypses. These books did not make it into the biblical canon, even though they claimed to have been written by biblical figures, such as Paul and even Mary Magdalene. Books claiming to be by or about biblical figures but not accepted into the canon are called *apocryphal* books. (This phenomenon also occurred among the Jews, for example, the apocryphal *Life of Adam and Eve*, which recounts what happened to the primal couple after God expelled them from

Eden.) The apocryphal gospels said much about Jesus' life, but some focused exclusively on his birth. A few of these infancy gospels contain absolute nonsense, but one had tremendous influence on Christmas.

In the middle of the second century a now anonymous Christian living in Syria wrote the *Protogospel of James*, claiming it was the work of Jesus' disciple James or possibly James the first leader of the Jerusalem community and a relative of Jesus. Moderns would call this work a "prequel," that is, it claims to tell us about events *before* the birth of Jesus, specifically the birth and upbringing of his mother.

So what does the *Protogospel* say and how did it impact the Christmas story? First, it provides the names of Mary's parents, Joachim and Anna (Anne). There is no way to tell if these names are accurate. Modern scholars do not accept them as authentic, but previous generations of Christians did. The Medieval church developed an extensive cult of Saint Anne.

The *Protogospel* also explains something else that puzzles many people—why so much Medieval and Renaissance art portrays Mary's husband Joseph as an old man. This began with gospel references to Jesus' brothers and sisters. Some modern churches believe in the perpetual virginity of his mother Mary, and they explain these brothers and sisters as relatives of Jesus but not full-blood siblings. This interpretation has validity since "brother" and "sister" are occasionally applied in ancient literature to non-siblings. But the author of the *Protogospel*, reflecting the views of the second-century Syrian church, took a different approach. He explained the brothers and sisters by claiming that Joseph had been married before. His wife had died and left him with children. Mary's parents had dedicated her to the Temple in Jerusalem, but when she became an adolescent and might have polluted the ritual purity of the holy place, the Temple priests decided to find her a husband. A miracle led them to Joseph, who identified himself as "an old man with grown children." He

married Mary, but they did not have relations, so the Syrian
Christians could account for the gospels' "brothers and sisters" and still insist on their belief in her perpetual virginity.

The devotion of the Syrian Christians to Mary's virginity
took another step forward. The gospels spoke of a virginal
conception, and other Christians shared the Syrians' belief in
her perpetual virginity, but the Syrians believed not just in a
virginal conception but also a virgin birth, that is, Mary gave
birth to Jesus with no change to her body, which remained an
intact, virginal body. This belief took quite a big step, but
slowly and surely other churches came to accept it. Since the
Middle Ages the Catholic Church has taught that Mary was a
virgin before, during, and after Jesus' birth, a belief expressed
in the Latin formula *ante partum, in partu, post partum.*

The *Protogospel* had even more to say. It tells us that Mary
was sixteen when she gave birth to Jesus, a reasonable esti-
mation for the ancient world when girls got married as early
as twelve and thirteen. It also says that Jesus was born in a
cave, not the stable of Luke's gospel. This notion grew in popularity, and in future centuries Christian pilgrims to the Holy
Land visited the "Cave of the Nativity." This apocryphal gospel also increased the significance of the star of Bethlehem,
claiming it shone so brightly that it dimmed the other stars.
The evangelist Matthew said nothing like this, but a fabu-
lously bright star became a staple of Christian art and, in the
modern era, of Christmas cards.

The *Protogospel* also added to the story of John the Baptist
and other gospel passages as well, although these did not become attached to the Christmas story.

But how could these Syrian Christians just write their own
gospel? Two reasons. First, as we saw, the Christians did not
finalize what books belonged in the New Testament canon
until the mid-fourth century, and until then the concept of
Christian "Scripture" did not mean a closed list of books. In
some ancient Christians' minds the *Protogospel* was a serious
candidate for the canon. Second, Christians have always

added to the Scriptures. Famous novelists such as Thomas Mann and Taylor Caldwell wrote fictional accounts of New Testament figures; movie directors such as Martin Scorsese and Mel Gibson added events and characters not found in the gospels in their films about Jesus; as for Jesus' birth, the composer Gian Carlo Menotti wrote an opera about a shepherd named Amahl who went to Bethlehem with the magi, while the songwriter Katherine Davis had a drummer boy visit Jesus. Christians have never been satisfied with what the New Testament provides, and they have been adding to the story of Jesus for almost two millennia.

But then as now, many Christians felt uneasy about adding nonbiblical material to scriptural stories, and they believed that they could add to the account of Jesus' Nativity and still stay within the Bible. From the time of Jesus' ministry, Christians understood that many passages in the Old Testament pointed to his life. In most cases they looked to actual prophecies, but they believed many other, nonprophetic passages also had importance. Surely, the Christians believed, some Old Testament passages pointed to the Nativity.

They soon found an important one, Isaiah 1:3: "The ox knows its owner, and the donkey its master's manger; but Israel does not know [God]." The early Christians identified the master as Jesus and then turned to the rest of the verse. The words "ox" and "donkey" appear often in the Bible, but the Christians focused on the word "manger" because of Luke's Nativity account. This Isaian passage did not tell Christians much about Jesus' birth, but it did change forever the visual image of that birth. Every pictorial representation of Jesus' birth includes the magi and shepherds, who are mentioned in the gospels, and also the ox and donkey because of this passage in Isaiah. The visual images also include sheep because of a Medieval tradition that the shepherds brought one or two lambs as gifts for the Holy Family.

In later centuries the Christians would again return to the Old Testament for information about the Nativity.

The Date of Jesus' Birth

The Christian interest in Jesus' life naturally included an interest in the date of his birth. Who today would study the life of George Washington or Jane Austen without knowing when they were born? So, when was Jesus born? Determining the year presented great problems. The Roman Empire officially used the Julian calendar, but many peoples in the empire, such as the Egyptians and the Jews, had their own calendars, which often caused confusion. The only real chronological information supplied by the gospels is that Jesus was born no later than the end of Herod's reign. When was that?

Today we use the B.C.-A.D. calendar, that is, Before Christ and *Anno Domini*, Latin for "In the Year of the Lord." In the sixth century a monk named Dionysius Exiguus created this calendar, but he made a rather serious mistake when he calculated that Jesus was born 753 years after the founding of Rome. Dionysius did not realize that according to his calculations Herod the Great died in 4 B.C., which produced an amazing phenomenon: Christ had been born four years Before Christ. So historians believe that Jesus was born no later than 4 B.C., but possibly two years earlier. Matthew tells us that Herod executed all the boys in Jerusalem who were "two years old or less," which means Herod thought, on the basis of what the magi had told him, that Jesus could have been alive for two years before the massacre of the Holy Innocents. That means he could have been born as early as 6 B.C. No more can be determined than that. This does present some confusion, but there is no real need to change the form of the calendar just for this.

What about the day? The gospels provide no clue as to the actual date, but that was not so unusual. Every year Christians celebrate Easter on a different date that falls within a general time period between mid-March and mid-April. This is because no one knows the actual date of Easter. The gospels tell us that Jesus died during a Passover week when Pontius Pilate was governor of Judea between 26 and 36 A.D., but no more than that. It is not possible to determine which Passover week it was since we do not know the year Jesus was born or how old he was when he died. Luke's gospel tells us when he began his public ministry he was "about thirty" (3:23), which could mean anywhere from twenty-eight to thirty-two. Furthermore, Matthew, Mark, and Luke mention one Passover while John mentions three, so was Jesus' public career one year or three? Recognizing these difficulties, by the mid-second century the Christians concluded they could not determine the actual date of Easter.

Shortly after this they came to the same conclusion about Jesus' birth but went on to contend that if they could not determine the exact date, they could determine an appropriate one. For example, the Christians often tried to replace a pagan feast day with a Christian one to alleviate the difficulties of conversion. In Egypt January 6 had a dual significance as a festival of the virgin goddess Kore and the birthday of the deity Osiris. By the second century, some Christians claimed this date for themselves, but in an unusual way.

From the time of the apostle Paul, Christians believed that Jesus had died a redemptive death on the cross for the sins of humanity. But in the second century, some converts with a Greek education had difficulty with that because the great Greek philosopher Plato had called the body the prison of the soul, and many Greek-educated Christians thought the body was too unimportant to be a means of redemption from sin. But if Jesus did not redeem humanity with his physical death, how did he do it? For these Christians, he did it by bringing us a secret and special knowledge.

The Greek word for knowledge is *gnosis*, and historians call these Greek-educated Christians "Gnostics." With a low opinion of the body, the Gnostics did not see January 6 as the date of his birth but as the manifestation of the divine Son of God on earth. The Greek word for "manifestation" is *epiphany*. For the Gnostics, Jesus' epiphany could have been his birth, but it also could have been his recognition by the magi, his acknowledgment by the Father at his baptism, or his first miracle, the changing of the water into wine at the wedding at Cana.

This is a very small beginning, but by the early third century in Egypt some Christians in Egypt celebrated a feast that could (but did not have to) refer to Jesus' birth. This date grew in popularity in the Eastern Mediterranean and represented a tentative step toward Christmas.

Other third-century Christians took a different tack. They looked for a date that would be symbolically appropriate. In the New Testament the apostle Paul refers to Jesus as the New Adam, and the book of Revelation used a lot of Genesis imagery, comparing the first creation to the new creation at the end of the age. By the third century some Christians ingeniously speculated that the New Adam had been incarnated, that is, created as human, on the anniversary of the creation of the world. But how did anyone know on what day God had created the world?

Actually, the answer was rather simple. The world moves through annual cycles, being born in the spring, flourishing in the summer, declining in autumn, dying in winter, and being reborn in the following spring. For many ancient people, the first day of spring, the vernal equinox and the first day of the regenerative period, marked the anniversary of the creation. Today we mark that day on March 20, but, according to the Julian calendar, the day was March 25. In the third century, many Christians thought Jesus' birth fell that day, a New Adam for a new creation.

But a North African Christian named Sextus Julius Africanus had a different idea. He contended that the Son of God became incarnate not at his birth but at his conception, so if Mary conceived him on March 25, he would have been born nine months later on December 25.

This, of course, is *the* day, but it did not catch on quickly. Yet it had much to recommend it besides Sextus's theology. The Israelite prophet Malachi had referred to the Messiah as the "sun of righteousness." Some early Christians applied that title to Jesus because Matthew's gospel says that at the transfiguration Jesus' face shone like the sun, and the book of Revelation says a figure "like the Son of Man . . . was like the sun shining" (1:13, 16). Early Christian writers picked up on that, and "sun of righteousness" became a common image for Jesus. (The phrase is still used today in the hymn "Hark the Herald Angels Sing.") This solar symbolism would play a significant role in elevating December 25 to be the date of Christ's birth, largely because of moves made by pagans.

By the third century the Romans had taken up an interest in solar monotheism. The emperor Aurelian (270–75), convinced of the futility of polytheism, instituted the veneration of one god, the Unconquered Sun, partly hoping that this new monotheism would help combat Christianity. During the same era many Roman soldiers and other men worshiped a virility god named Mithra, who was the son of the Sun. Both of these cults celebrated a great feast, the birthday of the sun, on the winter solstice since it is the shortest day of the year, and the sun grows stronger every day after that. The winter solstice, according to the Julian calendar, fell on December 25 (December 21 for us). Just as the Christian Egyptians had used January 6 to counter the feast of pagan divinities, so would the Roman Christians do with December 25.

But there was an added "bonus." The Romans celebrated a festival called Saturnalia, in honor of a pagan deity. The festival ran from December 17 to 23, and it involved much eating and drinking, gambling, temporary equality between slave and master, a mock king who presided over the feast, wearing of costumes including men and women wearing clothes of the opposite sex, and the exchange of gifts, although these were usually small things like wax candles. Much of this sounds familiar and would return as part of the secular Christmas, but it had religious importance for the pagans, and so the Roman Christian leaders hoped that their late December feast would counteract the pagan one and maybe keep Christians from taking part.

Barely a week after the end of Saturnalia, the Romans celebrated Kalends from January 1 to 5, greeting the New Year. For this festival the Romans decorated their homes with greens symbolizing the birth of the New Year, exchanged gifts, enjoyed temporary equality between the classes, and ate and drank a great deal.

Many people think that the church simply took over a pagan holiday, but that is not so. As Sextus Julius Africanus had shown, there were good reasons for celebrating the feast of Christ's birth on December 25, and sun and light symbolism played a very great role in Christian worship. By coincidence, this new feast could counter several pagan feasts, and while that added to its attraction, it did not determine the date.

Unfortunately we do not know who made the final decision to celebrate Christ's birth date on December 25, but no later than 335 it was being observed in Rome itself with the title *dies natalis Christi*, the "natal" (birth) day of Christ. We have Christmas.

CHAPTER TWO

Creating
the Christmas Season

The church at Rome now had a date for Christmas, but would other churches accept it? The Latin churches, those of Europe and North Africa, quickly agreed to the date, which had, after all, been proposed by a Latin scholar, the North African Sextus Julius Africanus. The churches of the Eastern Mediterranean had their own customs, and most used January 6 for the date of Jesus' birth, but that date could have other meanings, such as Jesus' baptism, the wedding at Cana, and the visit of the magi, so the Eastern churches were not absolutely committed to it. Additionally, those factors recommending December 25 to the Latin Christians recommended it to the Greek ones. In 379 the church at Constantinople, home of the Eastern Roman emperor, accepted the date; seven years later so did the important church of Antioch in Syria. Alexandria, leader of the Egyptian church and home of the original January 6 date, held out longer but accepted the date in 431. The oldest Christian church, Jerusalem, waited the longest, accepting December 25 only in the sixth century. But some Eastern churches never changed. For example, modern Armenian Christians celebrate Christmas on January 6, while the Russian Orthodox consider that date to be Christmas Eve and January 7 to be Christmas Day.

But a new question arose: what to do with January 6? The date had a long, honorable, and affectionate history for many

Christians, both Latin and Greek. Unfortunately we do not know the names of the people who changed the meaning of this date, but we do know that no later than 361 among the Christians in Roman Gaul (modern France) there was "the feast day in January celebrated by the Christians as the Epiphany," as a pagan historian reported. But how did the Gallic Christians observe January 6—in honor of Jesus' birth, of the coming of the magi, of his baptism, of the wedding at Cana, or even, as some Eastern churches were then doing, of the miraculous feeding of the five thousand? We cannot be sure, but we do know that by the late fourth century the church at Rome honored the epiphany as the coming of the magi.

The Romans made a good choice. Christmas depended upon the gospel infancy narratives, and the magi appear in Matthew's account. By settling on the coming of the magi as the epiphany ("manifestation") of Christ to the world, they had used the same gospel account that mentioned Jesus' birth and had thus kept the feast of the Epiphany in the orbit of the feast of Christmas. This decision made it easier for the Eastern churches to accept the new date for Christmas because it meant that they could keep January 6 as a date associated with Christ's birth. Slowly but surely the larger Christian community came to accept December 25 as the date for the birth and January 6 as the date for the arrival of the magi.

But the two dates had different histories. December 25 now reigned supreme as the feast of Christ's birth, but January 6 did not shed all of its other interpretations. Well into the Middle Ages Christians considered that date to be the date of Christ's baptism or the wedding at Cana or the feeding of the five thousand or even more than one of these. Modern Armenians still consider January 6 as the date of the baptism.

Now that the Christians had settled the date of Christ's birth, they turned to the hour he was born. We do not, of course, mean the chronological hour, which historians can never know, but an appropriately symbolic hour. Recall that the early Christians looked to the Old Testament for signs of Christ. The book of the Wisdom of Solomon (18:14-15) reads: "For while gentle silence enveloped all things, and night in its swift course was now half gone, your [God's] all-powerful word leaped from heaven."

"Half gone" meant the middle of the night or midnight. The Gospel of John and the book of Revelation both refer to Jesus as God's Word, so the early Christians naturally concluded that the passage in the book of Wisdom applied to Jesus who came from heaven at midnight. To them it seemed miraculously fitting that Jesus was born at the exact moment when time changed from B.C. to A.D. This tradition would eventually produce "midnight mass" as well as a host of legends.

Since the second century Christians had recognized the significance of Easter, which they honored as Christianity's most important feast, a place it still holds. But after the date for a feast honoring Christ's birth had been established, that feast rocketed in popularity, matching Easter and then taking some of the older feast's traits.

For example, the ancient Jews routinely fasted before important holy days, and the second-century Christians quickly followed suit, establishing a brief period of fasting before Easter. Slowly the period of fasting grew, picking up prayers and other modes of devotion, until by the fourth century it had evolved into the forty-day period known as Lent. It did not take long for Christians to conclude that Christmas also deserved a time of preparation known as Advent, from *adventus*, the Latin word for "coming" or "arrival."

The first known observance of Advent occurred in the late fifth century in the Roman province of Gaul. As with Easter, this preparation period would require fasting, in this case, on Mondays, Wednesdays, and Fridays during a forty-day period preceding Christmas, although the forty days excluded Sundays. Since this fast began on November 12, the day after the feast of the great Gallic saint Martin of Tours (d. 395), it

acquired the name, still used in France, of "Saint Martin's
Lent." Many Christian leaders considered this fast an appropriate preparation for Christmas, and it soon spread throughout all of France and into Spain, although with little
uniformity. But the forty-day fast was not universal. In addition to November 12, Christians in various churches began
Advent on September 24, November 1, and even December 1.
Finally Pope Gregory I (590–604), also known as "the Great,"
created an Advent of four weeks marked by four Sundays.
This gradually caught on, but for centuries in Western Europe
the observation of Advent varied in length as well as in de-
meanor. Advent should have produced a penitential mood
that countered the raucousness of the pagan Saturnalia, but
the old festival had a way of hanging on. (People hate to give
up holidays.)

But the Christmas religious season included more than Advent. The Gospel of Luke tells us that Joseph and Mary followed Jewish law and had Jesus circumcised on the eighth
day (January 1), thus creating the feast of the circumcision as
well as the octave of Christmas, an octave being an eight-day
period of religious celebration, a widespread practice in Italy
and North Africa for the feasts of martyrs.

Luke also tells us that Jesus' parents presented him in the
Temple at Jerusalem on the fortieth day, which would be
February 2, the feast of the Presentation, also known as
Candlemas because of a number of rituals involving candles,
such as blessing and distributing them as well as their use in
worship services. The church at Jerusalem first observed this
feast in the fourth century; the Western European churches
did not start to celebrate it until the seventh century.

Luke further recounts that the angel Gabriel told Mary that
her cousin Elizabeth was six months pregnant, meaning that
if, as the Christians believed, the annunciation had occurred
on March 25, John the Baptist would have been born three
months later on June 25. However, the ancient Christians
chose a meteorological method for choosing the date. If Jesus

were conceived on the spring equinox and born on the winter solstice, then John must have been born on the summer solstice, which then was June 24.

The twelve-day gap between Christmas and Epiphany established a celebratory period, the twelve days of Christmas, a time that did not really have religious significance but a social one in the Middle Ages when people were relieved from work for those days. The twelve days also included feasting and a widespread belief that evil spirits were abroad in the land. We know it best via the song, whose only words anyone ever remembers are "and a partridge in a pear tree." (A lot of people have heard that "The Twelve Days of Christmas" was composed by English Catholics to safeguard their beliefs in time of persecution. But this is just a myth since the song dates to the eighteenth century when the persecutions had ceased.)

By the late fifth century the Christians had appointed the three days after Christmas as feasts for Saint Stephen, Saint John, and the Holy Innocents. Stephen was a martyr in will and in deed; in Christian tradition, John was a martyr in will who suffered but did not die at Roman hands; the Holy Innocents, as Jewish children, could not be martyrs in will but certainly were in deed.

Finally, although we are in the ancient period, let us mention one more feast day, a Medieval one. No later than the twelfth century Christians considered December 24 to be the feast of Adam and Eve. Since Jesus was the New Adam and second-century Christian tradition proclaimed Mary as the New Eve, the original Adam's feast led directly to that of the new one. The feast, of course, is no longer observed.

The earliest Christians, like Jesus himself, were Jewish, and so they were aniconic, that is, they did not make images because the Jewish law forbade it. By the middle of the second century the majority of Christians were Gentile, and they began to shake off some of the restrictions observed by Jewish Christians. Art stood at the head of their list.

When the Christians set about making visual representations, they had a problem because no Jewish models existed. They quickly turned to pagan ones. The earliest images of Christ, found in the Roman catacombs, have him with the face and even the manner of Alexander the Great; not surprisingly, some portrayals of God the Father have him looking like Zeus. The apostles routinely appear clean shaven and in togas, the way most Roman men looked.

Since the first art appeared in the catacombs, which were burial places, it focused on themes related to death and resurrection, yet there were also pictures relating to the Nativity, usually with the magi. (As the only Gentiles in the Nativity narratives, the magi enjoyed much popularity with Gentile Christians.) The relation of the Nativity to death and resurrection is quite appropriate because, as we saw, the evangelists wrote their narratives as introductions to their gospels, which stress Jesus' public career and death. Furthermore, no matter how happy a holiday Christmas may be, the infancy narratives speak of homelessness (no room at the inn); persecution and death (Herod); refugees fleeing for their lives (flight into Egypt); and myrrh, a spice used to anoint corpses, including Jesus' body, according to the Gospel of John (19:39).

A wealthy Roman would want to be buried in a *sarcophagus* or large stone tomb, and many *sarcophagi* had artistic decorations on the outside. Christian Romans kept up this tradition, and, appropriately, the art had death and resurrection themes, often portraying Adam and Eve along with a Nativity scene, thus stressing the birth-death link as well as the cosmic significance of Jesus' birth, since he had undone the harm the first parents had done to God's relation with the created world. This was a prominent theme.

The art also reflects something else. Gentile Christians never felt comfortable with the notions of poverty espoused by the gospels, especially Luke, and very early on they began to raise the social status of the Holy Family. The *Protogospel of James* says that Mary's father Joachim was a very rich man; it also turns Joseph from a carpenter into a building contractor who constructs houses. Once this road opened up, it did not end until the Renaissance when Italian artists opted for realism over legend. By the fourth century the Christians portrayed Mary sitting on a throne (!) as the magi come humbly to visit her. Soon a crown followed the throne, and a humble woman of Nazareth was on her way to becoming a lady (*domina* in Latin), a positive title today, but in the ancient world a *domina* was an aristocrat who would have had nothing to do with a peasant woman like the real Mary. The setting followed the persons as Mary and Joseph lived in increasingly elaborate accommodations, sometimes even a palace-like building with columns.

(Let me note that I support the freedom of artists to portray the Holy Family as they like. The point is that visual portrayal and thus some of the veneration of the Holy Family moved rapidly away from the gospel account.)

But this art is not really "Christmas" art in the sense that we can be certain it was created for the feast of the Nativity. Possibly some of it was, but most likely pictorial representations of the Nativity became "Christmas" art only as the popularity of the feast continued to grow and spread, and even then we cannot be sure.

Alongside the visual art came music, initially a topic as controversial as the visual. The ancient Jews included music in their religious and secular ceremonies, and their great king, David, had played the harp. But in the first century of the Christian era, for reasons scholars have still not fully discerned, the rabbis decided that musical instruments should no longer be used for worship, and they relied instead on plainsong or chant without instruments. The Christians inherited this tradition and considered musical instruments to be pagan. Christian writers warned that listening to musical instruments would urge believers to immoral behavior and that this applied especially to women. Like the Jews, the early Christians relied on chant. Because this was the only music used in churches, it took on the name *a capella*, Latin for "from the chapel." Some extreme Christians wanted women to have nothing to do with even this kind of music!

Since music often played a liturgical role, we do have Christmas music, that is, music composed for the feast. The most famous is a Latin hymn, *Veni, Redemptor Gentium* ("Come, Redeemer of the Peoples"), composed by Ambrose, bishop of Milan, in the late fourth century. He gave his name to the form of chant used in the church of Milan. This work of Ambrosian chant had eight four-line stanzas, all heavy with theology. Since Ambrose was a bishop and this hymn was sung at Christmas services, we must be impressed by the theological acumen of his parishioners, for this hymn has none of the warm, emotional tone of later Christmas music but instead focuses on theological issues. Ambrose believed strongly in the superiority of virginity as a form of Christian life, and the first four stanzas refer to Mary's virginity. Writing at a time of controversy about the nature of the Trinity and person of Christ, Ambrose sang of the Divine Word, of the Son's procession from the Father, of the Son's taking on human nature, and, in stanza seven, of the traditional early Christian theme of Christ as the light that banishes darkness.

A Spanish poet named Prudentius (348–ca. 407) wrote "From the Heart of the Father," a ten-stanza hymn that focuses much on the divinity of Christ and his assumption of human nature but includes a majestic stanza (ninth) on the elements of nature, such as storm, stream, forest, and frost, banding together to praise the infant creator of the universe, imagery reminiscent of Matthew's star heralding the birth of Jesus.

The Gallic poet Sedulius (d. ca. 450) composed "From the lands that see the Sun arise," which stresses the humility of Christ's birth, often with superb imagery: "To shepherds poor the Lord most high, / The one great Shepherd, was revealed." Not well known today, these early hymns began what would become one of the chief characteristics of Christmas, its remarkable, often beautiful, music.

Since Christmas was a feast day, the early Christian bishops also preached homilies for it. In the Roman world, with limited means of communication, no one could advance in the government without the ability to speak well in public. This tradition of speaking excellence carried over into the church. Obviously not every bishop produced great homilies, but several produced some masterpieces. The best known to Western Christians was Augustine of Hippo (354–430), a North African who presided over his see for decades and who preached literally thousands of sermons in his lifetime. Such an impression did he make on those who came after him that several Medieval bishops recommended to their priests that, instead of trying to compose their own homilies, they should read something by Augustine to the congregation.

Augustine faced the usual problem of preachers—his congregation could range from young children to elderly people, from illiterates to the highly educated. But he always played up to the congregation, using carefully phrased rhetorical devices, filled with biblical imagery, that he hoped would move them:

> When the Maker of time, the Word of the Father, was made flesh, he gave us his birthday in time. . . . Man's Maker was made man that he, Ruler of the stars, might nurse at his mother's breasts; that the Bread might be hungry, the Fountain thirst, the Light sleep, the Way be tired from the journey; that the Truth might be accused by false witnesses, the Judge of the living and the dead be judged by a mortal Judge. (Augustine, *Sermons*, 107)

But Augustine's sermons show other traits. Most important, by his day the bishops had concluded that virginity was superior to marriage. Some radicals actually disparaged marriage. Augustine defended marriage as a good but insisted that it had far less value than virginity. Not surprisingly he focused on Mary when speaking about virginity. Recall that in the New Testament only the infancy narratives speak of Mary's virginity, so those biblical chapters that made Christmas possible also provided grounds for the superiority of virginity. "When the king of all nations was himself born, then the glory of virginity took its beginnings in the mother of the Lord, who was privileged to have a son and at the same time exempted from losing her virginity. . . . Mary was a virgin before she conceived, a virgin after she gave birth. God forbid that . . . in this flesh from which Truth sprung, virginity should have been lost" (Ibid., 57, 108).

Augustine used the Eve-Mary theme when discussing Jesus' physical birth:

> If he had not been born of a woman, women might have despaired of themselves; they would have been mindful of *their* first sin, of the fact that it was through woman that the first man was deceived; and they would have thought that they had no hope in Christ. He came then as a man to give the male sex special preference, and he was born of a woman to console the female sex. (Ibid., 26)

The Eden-Nativity link would continue to play a role in the understanding of Christ's birth right down to the nineteenth century.

Augustine also followed a Marian tradition that had been growing, especially in Syria, for two centuries, and that was the belief that Mary experienced no birth pangs when she gave birth to Jesus. The fourth-century Syrian Christian poet Ephraem and the Greek theologian Gregory of Nyssa both proclaimed this, and the Eastern Christians accepted it gladly. At first this seems like one more accolade given to Mary, but it carries a serious theological content. After Adam and Eve disobeyed God with their original sin, he imposed punishments upon them and their descendants, including labor pains for women. To say Mary had no labor pains is to say that she was exempted from one of the consequences of original sin. What we actually have here is the beginning of the later Catholic doctrine of the immaculate conception, the belief that Mary was free from original sin and thus of its consequences.

Returning to Augustine's sermons, we must recall that much preaching contains themes immediately relevant to the congregation, for example, the great recession that began in 2008 caused homilists at Christmas to remind people of Jesus' lowly birth in a stable and to urge them to help the poor at that time of year. In Augustine's day astrology provided a reliable guide for many people, even including Roman emperors. The Christians considered this rank superstition, and Augustine used the feast of the Epiphany to attack it:

> For Christ appeared, not under the star's rule but as its ruler. . . . The star did not cause Christ to live in a wonderful manner, but Christ caused it to appear in a wonderful manner. Nor did the star foretell the miracles of Christ; on the contrary, Christ produced it among his own miracles. (Ibid., 158)

Before leaving Augustine, we should note one other element of his sermons that would also have a long future—anti-Semitism. This appears early in Nativity accounts. In the *Protogospel of James* Mary tells Joseph as they approach Bethlehem that she sees two peoples, one rejoicing (Gentiles), the other weeping (Jews). Commenting on the Jewish scholars who determined for Herod and the magi that the Messiah would be born in Bethlehem, Augustine said:

> By the grace of faith, these unbelievers [the Jewish scholars]—themselves liars but truthful in spite of themselves—were to give information to the believers, drawing upon the Bible, that they carried on their lips but not in their hearts . . . after they had shown the Fountain of Life to others [the Magi], they themselves perished of thirst . . . these same men who pointed out Bethlehem . . . later were to deny Christ who was born there . . . and they were to kill him, not when he was still speechless but later when he was grown and spoke. (Ibid., 155–56)

This virus, which afflicted all Christian churches into the modern era, would grow as the feast of Christmas grew.

Let us end this chapter on a more upbeat note, the magi. Matthew's gospel says only that they came from the East and brought gold, frankincense, and myrrh as gifts for Jesus. Clearly such meager information would not do; the Christians needed to know more about them.

First they turned to the Old Testament. In a passage they applied to Christ, the prophet Isaiah (60:3) had said, "Nations shall come to your light, and *kings* to the brightness of your dawn." The Isaian passage went on (60:6): "A multitude of *camels* shall cover you, the young *camels* of Midian and Ephah; all those from Sheba shall come. They shall bring *gold* and *frankincense* and shall proclaim the praise of the LORD." With this passage the Christians associated Psalm 72:10: "May the *kings* of Tarshish and of the isles render him tribute, may the kings of Sheba and Seba bring gifts" (my emphasis). The phrase "gold and frankincense" clearly made the Christians think of the magi. Furthermore, where else in any of the gospels did anyone bring Jesus gifts? But Isaiah and the psalmist identified the gift givers as kings. By the third century North African Christians had begun to think of the magi as kings, a belief that would spread in the centuries to come. The Isaian passage also provides the magi with a mode of transportation, camels, now a staple of modern visual portrayals of the magi.

Another Old Testament passage provided the number of kings, thus filling in Matthew's account. In Genesis 26 three pagans come to the Hebrew patriarch Isaac and acknowledge that he has the Lord's favor. As the only son of Abraham and the bearer of God's promise to the people Israel, Isaac had become for Christians a type or symbol of Christ. An Egyptian theologian, Origen (d. 254), understood Isaac this way and so interpreted these three pagans who came to him as symbols of the magi who came to Christ. Thus the magi became three. Why did Origen do so? He did not say, but scholars presume he posited three magi because of the three gifts. As the magi grew in prominence, so did the star. Theologians and homilists made it the brightest star in the sky, then the largest star that had ever existed, then the brightest star that ever existed, and finally that it was so bright that it shone even during the day. (If this sounds familiar, it appears in "The First Noel": "and so it continues both day and night.")

So there were now three kings traveling on camels and following the brightest star that ever existed, but a huge question remained: who were they?

Surprisingly, the earliest known attempts to name them date only to the early sixth century, and they originated in Christian Egypt. An anonymous Alexandrian author says their names were Bithisarea, Melchior, and Gaspar. These names caught on quickly, and by the middle of the sixth century they appear, slightly altered, on a Byzantine mosaic in the church of Saint Apollinaris Nuovo in the Italian port city of Ravennea. Here the names are Balthassar, Melchior, and Gaspar. Balthassar would lose an "s," while Gaspar would appear more frequently as Caspar. Although these names are now traditional among Western Christians, the Eastern Christians had many, many other names, although, like the familiar three, all are purely imaginary. The Syrian church, which contributed so much to the growth of Christmas, claimed there were twelve magi and duly provided twelve names for them along with seven names for the shepherds who visited Jesus.

Where did the names comes from? Balthasar is almost certainly drawn from Belteshazzar, a Babylonian king from the book of Daniel. Melchior seems to combine two Hebrew words, *melek* for "king" and *or* for "light"; this makes sense since tradition named him as the king who brought the gold, bright and a gift for a king. Gaspar/Caspar may come from a variation on the name of an Indian king.

As we leave the development of Christmas in the Roman period and move into the barbarian world, let us look at a saint who played no role in the development of the religious feast of Christmas but who now dominates the secular holiday, at least for children. In the early fourth century the seaport of Myra in southwestern Asia Minor (modern Turkey) had for its bishop a man named Nicholas. Between 303 and 305 he was arrested during a persecution but survived. In 325 Nicholas attended a great council of Eastern Mediterranean bishops at a city called Nicea, honored by many Christian churches as the first ecumenical council. Nicholas died on December 6, although the year is unknown. We can be confident of the day of his death because Christians believed that the death of a holy person was a new birth in heaven, and they honored that date. It was also standard practice for local churches to keep records of bishops' deaths. By the fifth century, many Christians believed that saints in heaven could intervene in earthly life, and they prayed for their intercession. Myra being a seaport, many of those who invoked Saint Nicholas wanted help on dangerous voyages. As the saint became known as a patron of those struggling against violent storms, people concluded that he could help others in dangerous or seemingly hopeless situations, effectively making him patron saint of the helpless. As Nicholas took on the image of helper of the helpless, it was only natural that his care would extend to the most helpless people in any society, children. His image as the patron of children would make him the ideal basis for the nineteenth-century Santa Claus—a phenomenon that certainly would have horrified the real Nicholas.

CHAPTER THREE

Let It Snow!
The Dark Ages

Many basic elements of the feast of Christmas had come into place by the fifth century: the very existence of the feast, the canon of the New Testament that made the infancy narratives part of Scripture, the date, the first art and music related to the Nativity, a burgeoning collection of apocryphal tales, a liturgical season, and hymns and sermons that popularized Christmas among the people. Yet all this occurred while the Christians lived in the Roman Empire. By the end of the fifth century the Roman Empire in the Western part of Europe had ceased to exist, partly through internal decline but mostly because of Germanic invaders the Romans called "barbarians." These barbarians would change Christmas forever.

The word "barbarian" does not mean savage but rather "uncultivated" or "uncivilized," that is, neither Greek nor Roman. The barbarians had laws and poetic tales, but they were nonliterate peoples who depended upon oral tradition to preserve their culture, something Roman Christians had difficulty understanding. The barbarians constantly moved about Western Europe, and so they built no cities; architecture meant nothing to them. Their visual art was portable because it had to be carried from place to place, so they created no great statues. They generally had trouble just representing human figures. But these Germanic tribes represented much of Christianity's future, and their conversion involved both a clash and a mingling of cultures.

Roman provinces became barbarian states. Gaul became France, the kingdom of the Franks; Britannia became England, the kingdom of the Angles; northern Italy became Lombardy, the kingdom of the Lombards. From the fifth to the seventh centuries these migrating barbarians created a new Europe. They also created a largely pagan Europe, and the church had to send missionaries to work among the tribes. The Christian missionaries, coming from a Roman environment, had no doubts as to the superiority of their culture, but they quickly learned that the barbarians would adopt much Christian teaching to their own cultural norms. This adaptation included Christmas.

A festival that fell on the winter solstice was one thing in Egypt, North Africa, and the Mediterranean coastline in general, but in England, Germany, and northern France there was real winter, complete with snow, ice, the occasional blizzard, and short, dark days. There was no way the northern Christmas would completely replicate the Mediterranean one.

But before we leave the Mediterranean world, let us consider the last contributions made to the Christmas feast by the declining Christian Roman world.

As we saw earlier, in the sixth century Pope Gregory I set the time for Advent, the weeks of the four Sundays before Christmas. In 506 a council of bishops meeting in Agde in southern France urged Christians to take communion on Christmas; in 563 the council of Braga in Spain told the faithful not to fast on Christmas since it was a joyous day; in 567 a council at Tours in northern France required fasting during Advent (it had previously been just encouraged) and declared the twelve-day period between Christmas and Epiphany to be "a sacred and festive season" (Weiser, 35). In a move that would often be repeated in later centuries, the Byzantine emperor Justinian I (527–65) declared Christmas to be a legal holiday. He forbade any public business, even in his capital of Constantinople, and let people off from work. In effect, he had intruded the sacred into secular, but this presented no problem because at that time no one separated church from state, and citizens considered their monarchs to be sacred figures who naturally involved themselves in religious matters.

Since the Christian Byzantine Empire had survived in the Eastern Mediterranean, the popes had regular relations with Byzantium, and Byzantine ambassadors often resided in Rome. The Romans celebrated two Christmas masses, one at midnight, a practice dating to the fourth century, and one in the morning as, of course, they would on any Sunday or feast day. Many Byzantines venerated Saint Anastasia, whose feast day fell on December 25, so the popes added a third mass for the Byzantine diplomatic community but kept to the Western tradition of celebrating only Christmas on December 25, thus creating a third mass for the feast. This third mass began at dawn and was called the *Aurora*, the Latin word for dawn. The first mass was in the church of Santa Maria Maggiore, which claimed to possess the crib in which Jesus had been laid; the second mass took place in the church of Saint Anastasia, which the Byzantine diplomatic mission used as a court chapel; the third mass was at Saint Peter's basilica.

This practice of three masses caught on in Europe, although the number of services naturally varied with the size of a parish and the number of people in attendance.

(Although the mass in the middle of the night should technically be at midnight, the Roman church initially said it should be held *ad galli cantum* or "when the rooster crows." Since, however, roosters usually crow around 3:00 a.m., attendance could be sparse, and the Romans eventually moved it to midnight. Other Christian churches simply used midnight, although in Spain this mass is known as *missa de gallo*, "the mass of the rooster.")

The sixth century also witnessed the creation of the B.C.-A.D. calendar. Pope John I (523–26) asked a Balkan monk, Dionysius Exiguus, to calculate the date of Easter, an enduring problem in Christianity. Dionysius did so, but he used the prevailing Roman calendar based on the reign of the emperor

Diocletian (283–305), a violent persecutor of Christians. Dionysius resented that a persecutor had such influence on the Christian calendar, and so he set out to create a new one based upon the birth of Christ. As we saw in chapter two, according to his calculations, Jesus was born 753 years after the founding of Rome. But those same calculations would result in the death of Herod in 4 B.C., something Dionysius did not realize but later scholars did. He created a new calendar that ultimately changed how the Western world viewed time, although his calendar did not catch on right away.

The sixth century also saw the general acceptance of the now traditional names of the now traditional three kings. It also saw the end of many of the theological disputes of the previous centuries, some of which—mostly in the Greek East—raised the question of whether or not Jesus was actually human and not a divine being clothed in skin. Obviously, there could be no feast of Jesus' birth as a human if he were not actually a man. But this theological struggle never really affected the West, and further disputes along those lines meant nothing to the barbarians waiting to be converted.

Before getting to the barbarians and Christmas, let us recall that so much of what we recognize as Christmas originated in Syria, North Africa, and Egypt, so why are we now turning north? The answer is simple: the rise of Islam.

Although the prophet Mohammed (570–632) considered Jesus to be a great prophet, after his death, his followers created states that recognized Islam as their official religion and soon warred against the Christian empire of Byzantium in what was often a religious conflict. In the seventh century the Arabs conquered Syria, then Egypt, and then North Africa. As Muslims, they granted the Christians in the conquered territory the freedom to worship, but, for a variety of reasons over the centuries, the populations of these regions became heavily Muslim. For all their great contributions to the development of ancient Christianity, Syria, Egypt, and North Africa would play no significant role in its future development. Christianity would become a mostly European religion and Christmas a largely European feast, and for Catholics and Protestants, a Western one. For that reason, we turn north and west.

When the Christian missionaries arrived among the northern barbarians, they found a flourishing pagan religion, yet one far different from the pagan religions of Greece and Rome. The missionaries also found a major winter feast.

Because the barbarians did not write, accounts of their religion by the pagans themselves do not survive. Just the reverse; Christians wrote about it. Obviously they did not know northern paganism from the inside. Furthermore, they considered paganism a threat to barbarian souls and so wrote about it in critical tones. But enough survives to give an account of their winter feast.

Northern winters were long, and the days were short. Cold and darkness, two traditional symbols of death, haunted the northern winters and provided a huge contrast to the Mediterranean ones. But the northerners fought back against the cold and dark, and they did this partly by a life-affirming winter celebration known to us as Yule.

The word "Yule" may come from the Scandinavian word for "wheel," a symbol of the chariot driven by the sky god Thor, or it may just mean "feast." The pagans celebrated it on the winter solstice, not as just a happy feast but also a defiant one, challenging the power of the shadow world on the shortest and darkest day of the year.

Many people, even in modern societies, have a fear of the dark, but the northern pagans had good reason to fear it: all sorts of evil beings roamed the world during that time. These would include ghosts, witches, vampires, trolls, demons, and dead people who rose from their graves. Darkness represented danger, and so the pagans faced up to it by affirming life and warmth.

But the winter festival also had a practical purpose. As winter approached, farmers and herdsmen had to calculate how much feed they had for their animals for the upcoming winter. They also had to determine which animals would be too sick or weak to survive the winter, so that precious feed would not be wasted on them. Thus in late autumn farmers and herdsmen would slaughter sizeable numbers of domesticated animals, most of which were edible. But the pagans had no way to preserve the meat for very long, and so at the end of harvest there was a gigantic feast at which people ate better than they would for the rest of the year.

But they did not just eat. They drank. A lot. The crops had been harvested, and the northerners could make ale from it. So common and extensive was the drinking that a Medieval Norwegian king was said to "drink *jul* (Yule) even when he was away from Norway" (Forbes, p. 11). Furthermore, the northerners made a better grade of ale at this time of year, a forerunner of the special seasonal brews now so common.

Even these hardy northerners could not celebrate outdoors, and so the winter feast was an indoor one. But they brought the outdoors to their homes, decorating them with evergreens, signs of life even in the coldest of winters. Evidence suggests that local nobles would host the feasts, although the poor would also celebrate in their homes.

One aspect of the feast all could share because it cost nothing: the Yule log. People would cut down logs and bring them to their homes; the largest logs were used for communal celebrations. The log provided warmth and light, something desirable for the ghosts of those who had died during the year and who were believed to attend the festival one last time. The pagans would save a brand of the Yule log to light the new one when the feast came around again.

Much of this sounds familiar. That is because the Christian missionaries sought to convert the people away from their pagan deities but tried to preserve, where possible, elements of the culture, such as the Yule log, that did not challenge the faith. For example, on the first anniversary of a family member's death, Romans would have a meal at the gravesite and set a place for the deceased. This touching custom evolved into the Christian practice of remembering holy people, especially martyrs, on the dates of their deaths, and thus we have saints' feast days, such as December 6 for Nicholas. The missionaries in the north took the same approach to the local culture, thus unintentionally preserving what became some essential elements of the Christmas feast.

The period after the end of Rome is known as the Dark Ages, and in many ways darkness did indeed prevail. The urban empire was no more, and most of the barbarians were uneducated and illiterate. This meant that the Christian leaders could not win converts with elaborate theology, so evident in the writings of Ambrose and Augustine, but instead they used some basic ideas—creation, original sin and damnation, salvation in Jesus, heaven and hell, and, increasingly, the power of the saints to help people against evil spirits. What impressed the barbarians about Christmas was not just its relation to their own winter feasts, but also its spectacular elements such as the angels in the sky and the coming of the magi as well as the exciting story of the Holy Family's flight into Egypt, by this time a Muslim country totally exotic to the northern barbarians.

With few exceptions even educated people produced little in this era. Scholars knew that they lived after the great era of Christian theology and that they could not equal the formative minds of early Christianity. Many theological works rely mostly on quotations from the fathers of the church as the ancient writers were now called. This lack of originality extended to Christmas. No treatises survive that expanded it theologically, although the occasional bright note appears.

The brightest note was the Anglo-Saxon monk known as the Venerable Bede (673–735). Best known for his history of England in the Dark Ages, he also wrote commentaries on the Bible. Unlike many of his contemporaries, he liked the new chronology drawn up by Dionysius Exiguus, and Bede's work popularized the B.C.-A.D. way of reckoning history.

After Bede, historians generally took this form of dating for granted as they still do.

Bede also altered our understanding of the magi, not with his own originality but by settling a question that had been around for a century or two. By the fifth century, the magi were three in number; no one in the West challenged that even though the Bible does not provide any number. Matthew's gospel said the magi came from the East, which historically would have been Persia (modern Iran), traditional home of the magi. But many Christian scholars realized that the magi had a theologically symbolic value, signifying the Gentile world coming to recognize Christ. Augustine liked to make this point, so naturally later writers, like Bede, also paid attention to it. But there was a problem. If the magi represented the whole world, how could they come from just "the East," as the gospel says?

Christian theologians addressed this problem in a familiar way; they looked in the Old Testament. If the magi symbolized the whole world, were there any biblical antecedents? The only place where the Bible treats of the whole world is in the opening chapters of Genesis, so scholars looked there, and they quickly found what they were looking for.

After the great Flood, the three sons of Noah—Shem, Ham, Japeth—became the fathers of all humanity since Genesis makes it clear that all humanity consisted of just three races, the only ones known to ancient Israelites. Shem fathered the Semitic peoples since the Israelites were Semites and knew of other peoples (Babylonians, Assyrians) like themselves. Ham fathered the African peoples. How did the Israelites know about them? Some of their ancestors had been enslaved in Egypt, itself an African country and a place where the Israelites encountered several African peoples. Japeth fathered the Indo-Europeans, which by the sixth century A.D. meant those living in Europe. The Philistines who attacked Israel were Indo-Europeans, which explains how the Israelites knew about them.

Combining history and theology, Bede interpreted the three magi spiritually, claiming that they signified the three parts of the world, Asia, Africa, and Europe, that is, the entire human race that took its origins from the three sons of Noah (Trexler, 38). Bede's influence made this the accepted interpretation, and this is why Christmas crèches routinely show the three kings looking like the members of these three groups. "From the East" of Matthew's gospel faded into the background.

The barbarian fondness for simple stories over complicated theology also guaranteed that the apocryphal infancy narratives would enjoy much esteem. The *Protogospel of James* remained popular; people took for granted the existence of Saints Joachim and Anne as the parents of Mary while Joseph remained elderly in Christian art. Accounts of the Holy Family's stay in Egypt grew. The Dark Ages also produced a new and very popular apocryphal infancy narrative.

About the year 800 an anonymous Latin writer collected a group of diverse traditions into a work now known as the *Gospel of Pseudo-Matthew*, a somewhat clumsy title that derives from the author's claim to have been the apostle Matthew, a crude attempt to give the work legitimacy. It is a wonderfully preposterous book that is fun to read, as long as one does not take it seriously. "Pseudo-Matthew" realized the dramatic possibilities of the Holy Family's stay in Egypt. As Jesus and his parents travel along, dragons suddenly threaten them. Jesus pacifies the dragons, clearly symbols of evil borrowed from the book of Revelation. Jesus then assures his parents that he controls all animals, and he conveniently arranges for lions and leopards to accompany the Holy Family as bodyguards, so to speak, on their journey. This is an effective play on the notion of Jesus as the New Adam. Just as the original Adam lived in peace with the wildlife in the Garden of Eden, so Jesus does in the desert. Obviously the accounts of Jesus' overcoming the dragons and mastering the lions and leopards would have been exciting for illiterate peasants to hear.

Pseudo-Matthew uses another effective device, a contest of power. For some unexplained reason, the Holy Family, pious

Jews, decide to enter a pagan temple. The presence of Jesus causes all the idols to fall to the ground and split into pieces. The local governor rushes to the scene to avenge the "gods," but immediately realizes that Jesus is a divine child and worships him. The governor even warns his soldiers that if they try to harm the Holy Family, they will suffer destruction as did Pharaoh's army in the Red Sea! But this fantastic story does recall the biblical Matthew's comparison of Jesus to Moses.

Many legends and tales about Christmas also grew up among the peasants. One was that at midnight there was universal peace and even silence throughout the world, reflecting the belief that absolute silence was a traditional attribute of divine presence. Peasants believed that all was calm and all was bright and that heavenly peace ensued.

So awesome was this universal peace that even animals felt it. People believed that both domestic animals like cattle and horses and wild animals like deer fell on their knees at Christmas midnight. While no one takes this literally today, some Christmas cards still show animals kneeling at the sacred moment.

People living close to animals created even more legends about them. A Jewish tradition claimed that in the Garden of Eden, before Adam and Eve disobeyed God, animals could talk. Since Christ was the New Adam, many Medieval people believed that at midnight on Christmas Eve, the animals temporarily regained their ability to speak.

On a more serious note, many peasants believed that on Christmas Eve, all the evil spirits went into hiding, their spiritual darkness unable to bear the arrival of the sun of righteousness.

Educated people can smile at these stories today, but we must remember that they helped simple people to get through a difficult period of the year.

The symbolism of the new birth represented by Christmas appeared in the Dark Ages in several ways. On Christmas

Day in 598 the missionary bishop Augustine of Canterbury baptized hordes of Anglo-Saxon pagans; tradition says he welcomed ten thousand people to the new faith. These pagans became born again as Christians on the day of Christ's birth. In the later Roman period, the emperors were Christian. When the empire ended in Western Europe, it continued in the Eastern Mediterranean as the Byzantine Empire, but the popes, the bishops of Rome, never felt comfortable with the Byzantines. In the late eighth century the Frankish (French) king Charlemagne united most of Western Europe, including much of the old Roman Empire. Pope Leo III saw Charlemagne as the civic savior of Western Europe, and so, to the chagrin of the Byzantines, ruler and pope revived the Roman Empire in the West. The pope crowned Charlemagne emperor on Christmas Day in the year 800 on Christ's birthday, giving birth to an empire in the West, one that would survive in one form or another down to the twentieth century.

In the Dark Ages monks dominated not only much of the church but intellectual life in general. Much of the surviving art consists of illustrations in manuscripts, often biblical manuscripts with the story of Jesus' birth. Apocryphal themes abound, and the artists occasionally advanced their own ideas. A ninth-century French manuscript shows the slaughter of the Holy Innocents in a graphic way, but the artists added an effective detail: Herod is in Bethlehem, presiding over the mass murder.

In a world of Western Europeans, the Holy Family, the magi, the shepherds, all look like Western Europeans. A classic example appears in a ninth-century Irish manuscript known as the Book of Kells, which has an illustration of Mary holding a baby Jesus who has red hair and green eyes! But we still cannot be sure if this is Christmas art or more Nativity art.

Devotion to Mary grew significantly and became a regular part of the Christmas observance, often by herself but mostly with her son. Many illustrations show the magi (now, of

course, three kings) visiting Jesus and Mary (who is often on
a throne), but usually Joseph is nowhere to be found.

As a religious feast, Christmas naturally had liturgies. We
know of the three masses commonly said, but there was also
music. The chant of the earlier period, the Ambrosian chant,
faded in importance and was restricted to the Milan area
where Ambrose had been bishop. In the Western European
Latin churches, Gregorian chant replaced it.

Gregory I took an interest in liturgical reform and worked
to improve the music used in the church at Rome, but he did
not compose music himself. But the music used in Rome
traveled north into France during the reign of Charlemagne
(768–814), and much of what we know as Gregorian chant
originated there.

Like the earlier chant, this was plainsong, sung without
musical instruments. Since monks dominated so much of
early Medieval intellectual life, they composed music reflecting their life: plain, unadorned, well-ordered, and focused on
spiritual content. Following early Christian writers, the
monks had reservations about the emotional power of instrumental music.

Over three thousand pieces of Gregorian chant survive (not
all from this period) and they show that, contrary to what we
might expect, this music inspired creativity and, within lim-
its, diversity. Following the theories of early Christian writers,
the words predominated over the music. Today a composer
would match words and music for an effective sound, but the
words, especially those of Scripture, reigned in the Dark Ages.

In one sense, plainsong was monophonic, that is, just one
sound, but that did not necessarily mean that the chant was
dull. The cantors often sung antiphonally, that is, some
members of the choir would chant one verse while other
members would respond with another one. Singers could
modulate their voices, and a single syllable could be carried
through several tones. The text could be sung by an individual or by a group or by an individual and then by a group;

lines could be sung at different volumes as well. All of this
helped to avoid monotony. Finally, in convents, women could
sing the chant, reversing the earlier prohibitions against
women singing, although we have no evidence of singing at
services by the larger congregation.

No small reason for the widespread use of plainsong was
the lack of musical notation, which could guide the singers in
rhythm and pitch. In the middle of the ninth century neumes
appeared, signs to guide the singers in pitch, volume, or
tempo. In that same century we find in France evidence of
polyphony, that is, sounds sung simultaneously by different
singers, but this method would bear fruit when the Dark Ages
had passed into history.

This music of this period is not well known today, even to
professional musicians. The one piece of Gregorian chant everyone knows is "O Come, O Come, Emmanuel," which derives from a series of short prayers called the "O" antiphons
(because all began with "O"), which were used in Advent.
This series of antiphons dates to the ninth century, but the
familiar song dates only to the thirteenth century.

Instrumental music did exist but outside the church. Only
fragments survive, but we can be certain that secular celebrations of Christmas, for which evidence does survive, would
have included instrumental music.

This period also produced some fine poetry for the season.
In the ninth century an anonymous Anglo-Saxon author
composed poems entitled *Advent Lyrics*, which included seg-
ments on Christ's birth. The best known is a poem called
Christ I. Since the poem is in the Old English vernacular, it
was probably intended for an educated audience of churchmen and laypeople since it contains much theology. It focuses
on Jesus' birth as an answer to original sin: "now the Lord of
life / Must rescue from devils the droves of the wretched . . .
the Dark Spirit led us astray / Beguiled and seduced us
through grievous sin." The counter to the Dark Spirit is "O
Rising Sun! Most radiant angel / Over the middle-earth sent

unto men! . . . the bright sun . . . comes to illumine those
. . . sitting attired with darkness." The poem also refers to
the virginal conception and fulfillment of prophecies. Completely absent are any references to "the little baby" or other
sentimental touches; these would not really appear until the
Late Middle Ages (Kennedy, 28).

Homilies from this period also continue early Christian
theological themes, such as the emphasis on the birth of
Jesus as a counterweight to the harm done by original sin
and as a setback for the devil. The Venerable Bede, who popularized the B.C.-A.D. calendar, prepared many homilies for
Advent, Christmas, and Epiphany. Here are excerpts from a
Christmas homily on Augustus's decree that the whole world
should be enrolled:

> We must not suppose that this census happened by chance
> but rather that it occurred through a most certain divinely-
> arranged plan of this same Redeemer. . . . He himself
> granted that this time should be as he willed, that in a calm
> among the storm of wars a singular tranquility of unusual
> peace should cover the whole world. . . . He chose a time
> of utmost peace to be born in the world that he might lead
> the human race back to the gifts of heavenly peace. (Bede,
> *Homilies*, 52)

This is a fine play on the peace imagery, and note the reference
to leading "the human race *back*" to peace. This reminds humans that they once had perfect peace in the Garden of Eden
but lost it to sin. The New Adam theme continued to be strong.

A very practical man himself, Bede believed Jesus acted
practically:

> And we must not pass over that the serenity of that earthly
> peace, at the time when the heavenly king was born, not
> only offered testimony to his grace but also provided a ser-
> vice, since it bestowed on the preachers of his word the ca-
> pability of traveling over the world and spreading abroad the
> grace of the gospel. (Ibid., 52–53)

The secular celebration continued side by side with the religious one. Since this time of year still represented a break from the round of work in a primarily agricultural society, it always involved heavy eating and drinking along with public revelry. A German chronicle mentions "profane songs" being sung at Christmas. "Profane" does not mean gross or offensive—it just means "nonreligious"—but when we find clerics expressing disapproval, most likely more than the secular themes were involved.

While most clergy felt uncomfortable with the raucousness of the secular celebration, they understood that these celebrations derived from very old traditions. They also understood that a hardworking, lower-class population, often living in shoddy accommodations and laboring all day for some nobleman who looked down on them, needed to take a break and let off some steam.

But not everyone understood that. In 743 an English missionary bishop named Boniface wrote to Pope Zachary (741–52) about a disturbing report he had heard that "on the first day of January year after year, in the city of Rome and in the neighborhood of Saint Peter's church by day or night, bands of singers parade about the streets in pagan fashion, shouting and chanting sacrilegious songs and loading tables with food day and night, while no one in his own house is willing to lend his neighbor fire or tools or any other convenience." There are also "women with amulets and bracelets of heathen fashion on their arms and legs, offering them for sale to willing buyers. All these things, seen by evil-minded and ignorant people, are a cause of reproach" (Boniface, *Letters*, 81–82).

Boniface's informants had obviously stumbled onto a Kalends celebration for the New Year, still being celebrated in raucous style more than four hundred years after the Romans started celebrating Christmas. Zachary was not a Roman but a southern Italian of Greek ancestry who may not have realized how important this festival was to the urban populace. He assured Boniface that he had ordered the merriment to cease, but the Romans kept on celebrating. Later popes wisely, prudently, and generously allowed the winter festivities to continue. The festivals would both grow and spread.

The Dark Ages had one more legacy for Christmas, and it is a huge one.

In this period Advent was a period of fasting that lasted until people went to mass on Christmas Day. Not surprisingly, people anxious to end their fasts went to the earliest mass they could, the one at midnight. Because the gospel reading dealt with the birth of Christ, in England people began to refer to this mass, which began the sacred day, as "Christ's mass." Eventually this phrase became the name for the day and was soon shortened to "Christmas." Etymologists have found two instances of the word "Christmas" in the eleventh century, the earliest known uses of the word.

Thanks to the Dark Ages Anglo-Saxons, those of us who speak English have the name for our great feast.

CHAPTER FOUR

The Medieval Christmas

The High Middle Ages, the twelfth, thirteenth, and fourteenth centuries, conjure up images of three c's: castles, cathedrals, and crusades. We will add a fourth c: Christmas.

By the twelfth century, most of Europe had become Christian. Muslims continued to rule much of Spain, in parts of Scandinavia the remnants of paganism still commanded people's allegiance, and, of course, people sinned as vigorously as ever, but the Christian character of Europe could not be denied. This shines through most evidently in the art: the great stained glass windows of the Gothic churches, the magnificent manuscript illustrations, the abundant statues. Yet in spite of all this, we still cannot speak of "Christmas" art as a distinct form. Multifarious images of the Nativity survive, but rarely can we say that a particular piece was sculpted or painted specifically for the celebration of Christmas. The Middle Ages heavily emphasized the cult of the Virgin Mary (*Notre Dame* means "Our Lady" in French), and since almost all of what the gospels tell us about Mary comes from the infancy narratives, most images of Mary show her with Jesus. The absence of Joseph from most of the images suggests a non-Nativity theme, so we are probably not looking at works prepared for Christmas but rather images forming part of a constant Marian devotion that was independent of the feast.

But if we cannot be sure of the art, we can be sure of the liturgy, of poetry, of plays put on by the church for the laity, and of the Christmas music that grew considerably in this period.

The daily form of the liturgy did not change much in this period, although by the Middle Ages it was celebrated exclusively in Latin, which had become the preserve of educated clerics and perhaps a few laymen, although priests preached homilies in the vernacular languages. But the Christmas liturgical season expanded again, not as it did in early Christianity when it was created, but in the sense of filling in more days before and after the feast.

Fortunately we have a valuable Medieval source who testifies to this growth.

Jacob of Voragine (1230–98) was born in northern Italy. He entered the Order of Preachers (more commonly known as the Dominicans) in 1244, became a teacher and later an administrator. In 1292, at an age when most Medieval people had gone to their graves, Jacob became bishop of Genoa and established a reputation for kindness to the poor.

He wrote volumes of sermons and some historical works, but he is best known for *The Golden Legend*, a misleading title in English. The book includes accounts of saints who have feast days on the church calendar, and the original Latin title is *Legenda Sanctorum*, literally, "things to be read about the saints." "Legend" does not necessarily mean things that are untrue (although the book abounds with those). The book's popularity earned it the adjective "Golden."

The book contains little originality, which makes it valuable to us because it shows us what ordinary Medieval people thought and believed about the saints officially venerated by the church. Jacob generally listed them in the order of their feast days, thus Saint Stephen on December 26 and Saint John the Apostle on December 27. By the thirteenth century many saints' feast days had become associated with Christmas along with other days traditionally linked with that feast, such as the Epiphany. Jacob does not describe the actual liturgies of these days, but he does show us their links to Christmas. He also shows us how the myths and legends surrounding Christmas had also grown and been accepted not just by illiterate peasants but even by learned churchmen. Here is a brief survey of what Jacob tells us.

Just as the modern secular Christmas starts well before the holiday (September in American retail stores), so the Medieval Christmas started well before the feast with the first Sunday of Advent, especially in France, the great center of Medieval culture. Before and even after Pope Gregory I codified the four Sundays of Advent, different countries celebrated it in their own way. In France Advent started on the feast of Saint Martin of Tours (November 11), and the French called the season "Saint Martin's Lent," because both seasons required fasting. Martin had nothing directly to do with Christmas, but, like Jesus, he had cared for the poor and was willing to give up his life for his beliefs, although he never actually had to do that.

On November 30 fell the feast of Saint Andrew, one of Jesus' twelve apostles, about whom almost nothing is known except that he was the brother of Peter and one of the first to follow Jesus. Jacob gives a full legendary life of him, including his supposed martyrdom. Andrew also served as patron saint of Scotland.

But the next saint on Jacob's "Christmas list" now defines the day: Saint Nicholas, December 6. By the thirteenth century Nicholas enjoyed a widespread cult and had become a patron saint for children. Nothing yet linked him directly to Christmas, not even gift giving, but the cult of this saint who helped the helpless would do nothing but increase. Additionally, his cult's focus on children meshed well with the coming of the child Jesus.

Saint Lucy (December 13) lived in Sicily in the Roman period, but even though she was a historical figure, only legends about her survive. Scholars accept the tradition of her martyrdom by the pagans, but her name related her to Christmas. "Lucy" derives from *lux*, the Latin word for light. We can understand the importance of light as the days grew shorter as well as the link to all the light symbols of Christmas ("sun of righteousness"). She acquired an enormous following in the dark north of Europe, and to this day the feast of Saint Lucy inaugurates the Christmas season in Sweden, a country of few Catholics.

After Christmas come three feast days that are linked: Saint Stephen the protomartyr of Christianity on the 26th, John the Apostle on the 27th, and the Holy Innocents on the 28th. Jacob clearly explained this sequence. "There are three kinds of martyrdom: the first willed and endured, the second willed but not endured, the third endured without being willed. Saint Stephen is an example of the first, Saint John of the second, the Holy Innocents of the third" (*Legend* I, 50). The Acts of the Apostles tells us that a Jerusalem mob stoned Stephen to death. Medieval legends claimed that John had suffered for the faith and was willing to die but God preserved him. The Holy Innocents, all Jewish boys, died for Christ without knowing anything about him so that their martyrdom was "endured without being willed."

This sequence of three martyrs' feasts soon produced a fourth, that of Thomas Becket on December 29th. He was an archbishop of Canterbury who defied King Henry II of England and was murdered by some of Henry's knights in 1170. Pope Sylvester I's feast day fell on December 31 and had a tenuous connection to the infancy narratives since legend claimed that he had bested twelve Jewish scholars in a contest of erudition. The Jewish scholars and their number recall Jesus in the Temple at age twelve.

Protestants have always honored the saints as great Christians but have never accepted that saints act as intercessors between humans and God. Many modern Catholics, relying on a biblical spirituality, normally pray directly to God and do not go through the saints. But in the Middle Ages people believed the saints were very close to them and acted directly in their lives by helping with childbirth, illnesses, and a host of other matters. This help might be natural but could also be supernatural; God would perform miracles through his saints.

Thus a season filled with saints' days brought these powerful yet kindly people closer to everyone from peasant to noble and made the Christmas season a warmer one than it would otherwise have been.

Jacob of Voragine also gives accounts of the annunciation, the births of John the Baptist and Jesus, the Epiphany, and the purification of Mary in the Temple, all biblical events. He also includes an account of Mary's birth, taken from apocryphal material. He provides some good theology, again relating the birth of Jesus to the sin of Adam and thus to Jesus' defeat of Satan by his redemptive death, linking his birth and death as Matthew's gospel does. Jacob further uses traditional imagery, such as the sun of righteousness. But he also witnesses to the astonishing growth of legends and the indifference of Medieval Christians, even educated ones, to the biblical text. Thus Jacob can affirm with all confidence that Mary's parents were Joachim and Anna; that there were three kings named Caspar, Melchior, and Balthasar who rode camels; that Mary's birthing of Jesus was painless and occurred at midnight; and that a star shone during the day as well as the night. But Jacob adds material created after the early Christian period, such as that the magi were praying on a mountain when they saw a star that had the shape of a child inside and that the magi came to Jerusalem "with a numerous company" because Jacob knew that kings always traveled with retainers and courtiers. He reported that when Mary visited Elizabeth, she stayed until John was born and even lifted John from the earth with her own hands, which directly contradicts the Gospel of Luke, which says John's birth occurred after Mary had returned home. Not content to elaborate on Scripture, Jacob even elaborates on the apocryphal books. We learn that Mary's mother Anne had no fewer than three husbands (!), with Joachim, Mary's father, being the first.

These stories—imaginative and often exciting—actually make good reading, but the modern Christian can see the difficulty of subordinating God's word in the Scriptures to the fantasies of legend and myth. Yet this was the character of much of Medieval Christianity.

Another unfortunate and repulsive trait also shows up in Jacob's work, anti-Semitism. Several times he uses his accounts to "prove" the infidelity of the Jews, and not just in retelling biblical accounts but also in the saints' lives, such as that of Nicholas. But this, too, was part of the Medieval character.

One of the more remarkable elements impacting the Medieval feast was the use of plays to get biblical accounts across to the mostly illiterate laity. But these plays were not just catechism lessons. Many of the playwrights were gifted artists, and their work, intended for an audience that spoke only the vernacular, marks some of the earliest known literary works in English, French, German, Italian, and Spanish. We will focus on the English plays.

Religious drama in Latin originated with the clergy acting parts of the liturgy, much the way many churches conduct the Good Friday liturgy. Different members of the community would read different roles, so that one person would be the narrator, one would be the voice of an angel, and the like.

Here is a description of a Christmas drama from twelfth-century France:

A part of the sanctuary would be set off by a curtain as the stable in Bethlehem. The clergy would process into the church, singing "Let us go to Bethlehem." A boys' choir would sing the words of the angels from Luke's gospel, *Gloria in excelsis Deo, et in terra pax hominibus bonae voluntatis.* Two priests would ask those in the procession, "For whom are you searching?" They would reply, "Our Savior, Christ the Lord." The two priests would then open the curtain and point to an image of Mary and Jesus. All would bow reverently and sing hymns honoring Jesus and his mother. After this midnight mass would begin (Weiser, 94–96). As moving as this ceremony would have been, it was brief and, being in Latin, was not very accessible to the laity.

Soon the clergy realized that reenacting the biblical accounts for the laity would be an effective teaching method, but, of course, the plays could not be in Latin. The shift to the vernacular was not difficult since the clergy already preached in the vernacular and in so doing often recounted the biblical stories.

But plays can be complicated and require a lot of preparation. Furthermore, people could not just take a few hours off from work to see a play. Church leaders thus decided that they would stage a number of plays on a single day, with no play being more than twenty or twenty-five minutes long, and some were less than ten minutes. In this way people could learn about a number of biblical narratives. Furthermore, there would be no need for multiple preparations every year, while costumes and scenery, such as they were, could be stored and reused. In larger towns the churches created a cycle of plays that literally went from the creation of the world to the Second Coming.

This sequence did not attempt to cover large swaths of the Bible but instead to concentrate on biblical stories that had the most relevance to the people, so church leaders focused on the redemption of humanity by Jesus. Although there were many local variations, the sequence started with the creation and the Fall, followed by accounts of Old Testament figures who, in the Christian understanding of Scripture, pointed to the coming of Christ. Next came the infancy narratives from the annunciation to the return of the kings to their homelands and occasionally to Jesus in the Temple at age twelve. The plays next turned to Jesus as an adult, but little was done on his public career, the focus instead being on his suffering and death. Finally came the resurrection, post-resurrection appearances, accounts of Jesus' first disciples, and then the ascension.

The limited focus would disappoint many modern educated believers who know how much more there is in the Bible, but we must remember the audience. Almost all were illiterate—many were bright, but still illiterate—and they could not follow up on what they heard in church by reading a book such as this. Since farm animals do not respect holy days, the people had little leisure time, and the local church had to cram much into a brief amount of time. Finally, people are Christian because they believe that Jesus Christ redeemed us from sin, so the focus on the redemption was appropriate if there was not time to do much else.

Since the plays cost money to put on, the town churches usually worked with local guilds, such as bakers, tailors, and shearers, to share the cost and to get some workers. The guilds would choose members to sponsor one or more plays as well as to act in them. Sometimes the actors were topic-appropriate, that is, the goldsmiths would play the three kings who brought Jesus gifts. Guilds usually had a governing corporation, which would oversee the project in conjunction with local clergy.

To fit everything in, the plays would start at sunrise (in northern England that could be as early as 4:30 a.m.), and they would finish in the dark to the light of torches. Since these were annual rather than permanent affairs, no permanent theater buildings existed. Instead the plays were given on large carts and wagons, which in England were called "pageants." The organizers could wheel these out to the spot where the play would take place. Sometimes the wagons had two stories so that an angel could descend from heaven. The use of costumes varied; sometimes actors wore them, other times they wore contemporary clothing.

In order to reach the people, the writers simplified the biblical elements. For example, characters speak openly of the Trinity, a word that does not appear in the Bible, but to Medieval Christians the phrase "Son of God," which does appear in the Bible, would make little sense without the Trinity. The Jewish priests are designated "bishops" and were even dressed like them since the populace knew little or nothing about

Judaism, but the word "bishop" let them know a particular character held an important religious office.

The plays were usually performed on the feast of Corpus Christi, that is, the Body of Christ, which originated in the thirteenth century. Corpus Christi falls on the Thursday after Trinity Sunday, which is the first Sunday after Pentecost. This meant that the plays were performed in relatively good weather in the late spring. Then why include them in this book? Because when Christmas arrived, the people approached it religiously with the knowledge they had gained from sermons but also with the visual imagery they had gained from the plays. As psychologists (and media consultants) have repeatedly proven, the visual makes the greatest impression. The people understood much of the biblical accounts in terms of the plays that they saw. It would have been better to have the plays given close to the feast, but putting on a play outdoors in December has obvious drawbacks.

Who wrote the plays? Since normally only clerics could read, scholars assume that they wrote the first ones, but by the fourteenth and fifteenth centuries, as economic activity grew in towns, some businessmen (except for nobility, women were excluded from education in that era) and others learned to read and write. Proof of this lies in some great works of literature, such as Dante's *Divine Comedy* and Chaucer's *Canterbury Tales*, both written by laymen in the vernacular and which presumed people who could read Italian or English. Most likely the plays had both clerical and lay authors.

Their initial efforts were naturally awkward, but inevitably, as time went on, the playwrights gained experience, maturity, and confidence, and they began to produce better plays, some of which stand as monuments of vernacular literature.

The plays had a pedagogic function, teaching the biblical accounts to the laity. But, as we have seen, "biblical" accounts of the Nativity had grown significantly by bringing in apocryphal themes and pious speculation. In addition to the gospel basics, the plays would tell people there were three kings,

Jesus' maternal grandparents were named Joachim and Anne, and a star outshone all other heavenly bodies. The kings travel with sizeable retinues because people living in monarchies expected kings to travel that way.

Theological notions also appeared. For example, when the early Medieval theologians concluded that the three sons of Noah, founders of the three (known) races of humanity, symbolized the three magi, then the magi also represented the three races. But if that were the case, they would not have all been living in the same country when they first saw the star. Thus grew up the Medieval tradition that the three started from different places and met a few miles outside Jerusalem, where they all joined together and went to visit Herod.

Theology also appears in the references to Jesus as the Second Person of the Trinity and to Mary's perpetual virginity and her painless birthing of Jesus. But the theological themes also include biblical ones, especially the notion of the New Adam. Plays began with an Isaian prophecy that Jesus would undo the work of Satan, and Mary would comment upon how peaceful are the stable animals, recalling the Garden of Eden when humans and animals lived together in peace.

Local and Medieval themes abound. For example, in England the plays refer constantly to the cold weather. Since the peasants knew little about ancient Judaism, the Jewish elders and priests, as we just noted, became bishops, and synagogues became churches. Further proof of the Medieval ignorance of Judaism, we find that Herod worships Mohammed (often spelled "Mahound") because the peasants knew that the Muslims were a faraway people with whom the Christians fought in the land of Jesus' birth, and, like even many educated Medieval Christians, they believed that Muslims worshiped Mohammed as a deity. In defense of the playwrights, anyone who has seen a "historical" movie about the Crusades or Henry VIII knows how often modern writers defer to popular attitudes rather than historical accuracy.

Many plays show dramatic maturity. Villains often move plots better than the "good guys," and so Herod got his own plays, which usually start with a monologue by him, relating how much of the world he governs (including India and Turkey, just names to the audience). Medieval people, at the mercy of monarchs and nobles, would enjoy seeing a braggart lord like Herod arrogantly assuring the audience that he has now taken care of this threat to his reign when they know that the humbly born Jesus would survive and that Herod would pay the price for his actions.

But a truer image of the play's dramatic maturity lies in the treatment of biblical figures who play a minor role either in the biblical account or in the theology of the Nativity but with whom the audience could identify. At the head of the list came Saint Joseph.

By the High Middle Ages Marian devotion had grown enormously, and countless images survive of Jesus and Mary but without Joseph, while many Nativity images that do include him show Joseph off to the side or even sleeping. This resulted from the belief in Mary's perpetual virginity; the artists wanted to make it visually clear that Joseph had absolutely nothing to do with the birth of Jesus. But many in the audience were laymen who could empathize with Joseph, and the playwrights seized on a dramatic moment—Joseph's learning that Mary was with child.

In more than one play Joseph berates himself as an old fool who should have known better than to marry a young woman since no old man can ever trust a young wife. He complains of his gullibility and decides to leave Mary, swearing that he will never make a mistake like that again! Immediately after this decision, an angel appears to Joseph and tells him what really happened. Joseph promptly seeks out Mary and apologizes to her. It is a very dramatic and realistic scene that, of course, would have been inappropriate in the gospel. Also note the apocryphal portrayal of Joseph as old.

Another episode that captured the imagination of the playwrights and their audiences was the massacre of the Holy Innocents in Matthew's gospel. Matthew focuses on the escape of the Holy Family and the fulfillment of a prophecy, but many audience members were married and parents, and half of them were women who sympathized with the mothers of the Holy Innocents. Several plays included scenes in which the mothers plead for some time with Herod's soldiers not to kill their sons; after the killings the mothers express their laments in tears and wailing. When done well, this must have been a very effective scene.

To their great credit, the playwrights also gave an understanding treatment of Herod's soldiers who enlisted to protect the king and the people, not to kill babies. They protest to Herod in Medieval terms, pointing out that killing children was not only barbaric but went against their honor. But they also had a sworn duty to their liege lord Herod who was not above threatening them and their families, and so they carried out his orders.

These brief, effective plays are rarely performed today outside of universities, and even there the actors often use Medieval English, which a general audience would not understand. But, in their day, the plays helped the Christian populace not only to understand the facts of the infancy narratives and the legends surrounding them but also to see the biblical personages as true human beings with motives and feelings and concerns that went well beyond theological ones.

Literary artists wrote more than plays; they also wrote poetry. Most of it focuses on the Nativity, but toward the end of the Middle Ages (fourteenth and fifteenth centuries) we begin to find poems that relate to the Christmas feast. Many were written in Latin by educated clergy, but some survive in the vernaculars, including English.

Not surprisingly, given Medieval Marian piety, many poets emphasized Mary's role, such as a fifteenth-century lyric, "I sing of a Maiden," which interweaves Mary's virginity and motherhood. A fourteenth-century poem compares Mary to a rose and her son to a flower who would "break the Devil's chain of woes," maintaining the centuries-old emphasis linking the Nativity with the redemption. Another anonymous poem portrayed Mary weeping because Jesus' cradle reminded her of a bier, that is, the frame on which a coffin was placed. Babies often bring out sentiment in people, so we find poems lamenting the impoverished situation of the baby Jesus, sharing a stable with animals. Finally, one poem, urging people to gather together to rejoice in their friendship with Jesus, brings in a communal note. (The texts of English Christmas poems can be found in Stone, *Medieval English Verse*, 25–31.)

Since Christmas was a religious feast, its celebration involved hymns. The Middle Ages produced a large number of Christmas hymns, many in Latin, some in the vernacular. But for the actual liturgy in the churches, Latin was the only language.

The Medieval composers produced some beautiful Latin hymns, including one known to the general public, *Veni, Veni, Emmanuel*, translated into English by J. M. Neale (1818–66) as "O Come, O Come, Emmanuel." This slow, reverent yet melodic piece is probably the only work of Medieval chant that anyone has ever heard of. As we saw, the words appeared in earlier centuries as a collection of antiphons, the "O" antiphons, but the melody, by an anonymous composer, dates to the thirteenth century. Rather surprisingly, the beauty of this hymn has never inspired many people to look at other Medieval Christmas hymns that might enrich the celebration of the feast. I suspect this is because people think that chant must be monotonous and thus dull, but Medieval composers and singers could do much to bring variety into chant. Yet by the twelfth century composers in urban churches and even monasteries wanted some newer, more diverse music.

In that century composers began experimenting with homophony and polyphony. Homophony means that one voice primarily carries the melody, while other voices provide accompaniment to the vocalist by supplying color and blocks of harmony to support the lead vocalist. This produces the effect of a single melody with chords providing texture. But polyphony marked a crucial change. Now several voices and instruments combine to produce different sounds that often include counterpoint to one another. This approach gained popularity within the church in the thirteenth century.

The acceptance of polyphony and instruments did not mean an abandonment of Gregorian chant nor of the dignity and sacredness that this chant provided, but it did mean that church composers could experiment along new lines. Inevitably some of this experimentation occurred during major feasts such as Christmas.

Naturally the new music kept many of the traditional themes because devotion did not change, even if the music did. Emphasis continued to fall on the Virgin Mary, on the fulfillment of prophecies, and on Jesus' birth as our liberation from sin. But now we see more hymns using the theme of rejoicing (*gaudemus*, "let us rejoice") and praise (*laus*) as the music became livelier and more vivid. From the fourteenth century in northern Italy come hymns using words (in Latin) expressing joy and harmony; an English carol sings of Joseph buying a crib and Mary breastfeeding Jesus; a popular German song speaks of joy; a late Medieval hymn of undetermined origin says that "On this day the earth shall ring / With the song children sing." The new music allowed for a wider range of emotions, and composers took advantage of that.

Since the liturgical dramas had demonstrated the effectiveness of the vernacular, we find in the late Middle Ages a number of vernacular Christmas hymns, some of which are still sung today. They appeared in all European languages; we will look at some English ones.

Since vernacular songs were accessible to the laity, they contain themes of interest to the laity. One fourteenth-century song, "Als I Lay on Yoolis Night" ("As I lay on Yule night"), has an unnamed narrator tell of a vision she/he had of Mary singing to Jesus to help him sleep. A fifteenth-century carol also uses the first person, but now in the plural, "Be that rose (Mary) that we may see"; so does "Nowel syng we bothe al and som" ("Now sing we both, all and some"), recounting that "A boy-child was sent to us." Sometimes the personal involvement became specific as in "We happy hirdes men (herdsmen)" as the singers took the role of the shepherds of Bethlehem and identified them with the shepherds of England.

In the late Middle Ages something else makes an appearance in the songs, the feast of Christmas itself. "Make we joy now in this fest" has verses borrowed from religious songs that focus on the Nativity, but it refers directly to the day that observes the Nativity. Richard Smert (1428–77), a priest at Exeter Cathedral, wrote a carol entitled "Nowell: God keep you, fine sir," that speaks of "Syre Cristes masse," that is, "Sir Christmas," a personification of Christmas Day and possibly intended for a ceremony in which someone personifying Christmas would make an appearance. Smert, who seems to have led a rather active social life for a priest, also wrote "Nowell: The Borys hede (boar's head)," probably for a Christmas feast for the choir of Exeter Cathedral. King Edward II (1307–27) opened the boar-hunting season from Christmas to Candlemas, and, until hunted to extinction in the seventeenth century, boars formed a central part of the Christmas feast. It was common for servants to carry a boar's head into the dining hall to the accompaniment of songs written for the occasion. Smert did, however, use the line "The boar's head that we bring betokens [that] a prince without peer is born this day." (Maybe this is too far back for me to understand, but a decapitated boar's head with an apple in its mouth as a symbol for the Christ Child?)

Like the Gregorian chants, the music of this period should be better known; it is available only in specialized recordings. But one song has achieved popularity, "The Coventry Carol." This appeared in a play among the cycle of plays performed in the town of Coventry on the feast of Corpus Christi. By the end of the Middle Ages, when the play had faded, the song had taken on a life of its own. This tender piece is sung by the mothers of the Holy Innocents, weeping over their children and in their distress singing to them—"Lullay, lullay, thou little tiny child." The song can still move us today; when performed in a play that showed the soldiers killing the children, it must have had considerable dramatic effect. While it can move anyone, it would have especial meaning for mothers who had borne children. A vernacular carol with a particular message for women—that alone would make it unique.

Finally, the Middle Ages changed the way we view Christmas, literally.

Scholars debate about how early Christians may have put up Christmas crèches, but everyone knows who popularized them.

During the Christmas season of 1223, Francis of Assisi was preparing for the sacred feast in the Italian town of Greccio, where he had a friend, Giovanni Velitta, a local nobleman. Two weeks before Christmas Francis told Velitta that he wanted to celebrate Christmas by reenacting the birth of Jesus and by showing people how humble his birth had been. Francis planned to put a statue of Jesus in a manger with hay and to have an ox and an ass standing next to it. Velitta agreed and made the arrangements. Francis's biographer, Thomas of Velano, reports that "Greccio became a new Bethlehem." The people loved this new form of devotion, and Francis, a deacon, gave a sermon about the lowly birth of Jesus. Francis, himself the epitome of humility, took a great step toward humanizing Jesus in an era when artists routinely portrayed a crowned Mary, sitting on a throne with her royal child in her lap, often with the three kings bowing in obeisance. No monarchy for Francis but rather the humble baby and mother of the gospels.

Francis enjoyed mixed success. Many churchmen ignored him and continued to have artists portray Jesus and his mother as royalty, but the people loved the crèche, which became a central element in the observation of Christmas, although usually with statues instead of live animals.

The end of the Middle Ages also provides evidence of another important development, the growth of the secular feast. As usual, most of the evidence comes from the royal and noble courts, but it is substantial. Henry III of England (1216–72) once had a Christmas feast so large that his guests devoured six hundred oxen. During the reign of Edward III (1327–77) plays, and not always religious ones, were performed at court in the Christmas season. During the reign of his son, Richard II (1377–99), 130 mummers (people in costumes) came to the royal court for one Christmas. The mummers had dressed up as knights, cardinals, and visiting foreign princes. They brought the king gifts, played dice with him (and always let him win), enjoyed much food and drink, danced for a while, and then paraded out. Obviously average townspeople, much less peasants, could not celebrate in such splendor, but monarchs and nobility set the tone for the rest of society. They made it clear that celebrating Christmas can include gifts, heavy eating and drinking, games, and costumes, but, very importantly, they continued to celebrate a religious Christmas as well. Like most Christians, they did not see a conflict between the two.

CHAPTER FIVE

Reformation and Rejection and Recovery

At the end of the Middle Ages, tensions were building in European Christianity. In the eleventh century the Western European church had split from the Eastern one, which went on to form the Orthodox churches; several attempts at reunion fell short. Now a split would come to the West, and it would impact the feast of Christmas along with so much else.

A German monk named Martin Luther (1483–1546) concluded that the sole source of revelation and thus of authority in Christianity is the Bible. This put him at odds with the Roman Catholic Church, which taught that divine revelation can be found in the Scriptures and also in the traditions of the church, both to be authoritatively interpreted by the popes and their appointees. Initial attempts at reconciliation failed, and the Protestant Reformation began. It spread widely in Germany and Switzerland as well as into Scandinavia and the Low Countries; the Mediterranean countries, such as Italy, Spain, and France, stayed with Roman Catholicism as did parts of German-speaking Europe, such as Bavaria and Austria. Initially the Christians of Eastern Europe proved receptive to Protestantism but finally remained mostly Catholic. Protestant churches other than those following Luther soon arose, and the movement initiated by the French theologian John Calvin (1509–64) had a wide following. Joining the Catholics and Protestants came the Church of England, founded by King Henry VIII (1509–47) and the English bishops, which soon developed a distinctive theology and organization, becoming the country's national church. But in the British Isles, the Irish remained largely Roman Catholic while the Scots became Presbyterians (Calvinists).

Historians have focused on organizational and theological differences among the churches, but what believers noticed most were the changes in worship, for example, liturgies in the vernacular, retention or removal of stained-glass windows in churches, the types of prayer and of prayer books, and those presiding, such as celibate priests and married ministers. Inevitably the Reformation would impact Christmas.

The Protestant emphasis upon the Bible and the rejection of tradition as authoritative required people to know the Bible, which they could only do by reading it. Protestant leaders strongly held that believers should do this to be good Christians, but they also knew that Bible reading would demonstrate that many things taught and practiced by the Catholics could not be found explicitly within the Bible, thus supporting the Protestant position on authority. While this presented no problem to Catholics for whom church teaching shared authority with the Bible, it did demonstrate to Protestants how much of the traditional picture of Christmas did not appear in the gospel infancy narratives.

Protestants who read the Bible discovered that the gospels did not provide the names for the parents of Jesus' mother Mary, and devotion to Saint Anne, quite prominent in Medieval Catholicism, withered away among Protestants. Protestants also learned that there were only magi, not three kings, and that the stories about the Holy Family in Egypt were simply legends. This proved a bit of a shock for many people. Christmas is a traditional holiday, and people hesitated before giving up Christmas traditions. Yet Protestant leaders set out not to destroy extrabiblical traditions so much as to have people know what was actually in the Bible and what was not. Protestant families continued to use the name Anne for their daughters, and the "kings" continued to be three. But the most elaborate stories, such as those recorded by Jacob of Voragine, did fade. Furthermore, Catholics, stung by Protestant criticism that they had trampled over the Bible with nonbiblical myths, kept some traditional elements, such as Saint Anne, but they gradually downplayed some of the more extreme accounts. Not wanting to look as if they were giving in to Protestant criticism, Catholics did not totally abandon the accounts of Jacob of Voragine but instead cited them as "according to tradition," thus making it clear that the stories would not be found in Scripture.

Other new practices would change Christmas. By the fourth century Western Christians had gotten in the practice of asking saints to intervene with God on their behalf. Probably the best-known example of this is Saint Christopher, an early Christian martyr who, according to legend, carried the child Jesus across a stream; he became the patron saint of travelers. Another popular saint was Saint Blaise, also an early Christian martyr, a protector of people from afflictions of the throat, including fish and animal bones. Countries had their patron saints, such as Saint George for England, Saint Andrew for Scotland, Saint Patrick for Ireland, and Saint Denis for France. (No one ever explained what happened when two of these countries warred against one another and both sides asked for saintly assistance.)

But Protestants argued that invoking saints cannot be found in the Bible, which says (1 Tim 2:5) that Jesus Christ is the only intermediary between God and humanity. The Protestants soon abandoned the cult of the saints, so central to Catholic tradition.

How did this impact Christmas? By the sixteenth century the cult of Saint Nicholas had grown to enormous proportions, and we have evidence of children in Italy and France hanging up stockings on the eve of his feast and finding presents in them on the morning of December 6. Protestants abandoned his cult as part of their general turning away from the saints as mediators. Nicholas continued to be venerated by Catholics, but, with much irony, a nineteenth-century American Episcopalian would turn Nicholas into Santa Claus and move his gift giving to Christmas Eve.

Of all the intercessory saints, Mary was the greatest. As we have often noted, Marian devotion was enormous in the Middle Ages. It simply grew and grew in the Catholic Church, peaking in the nineteenth century when, in 1854, Pope Pius IX pronounced the doctrine of the immaculate conception, that is, the Virgin Mary's freedom from the guilt of original sin, which we first encountered in Christian Syria in the second century. The contemporary Catholic Church venerates Mary as the *mediatrix* (Latin for "female mediator") of all graces, officially making her foremost among the saints.

But none of this appears explicitly in the gospels. Although the Protestants honored Mary as the mother of Jesus, they downplayed her role as an intercessor, and Marian devotion plays little or no role in many Protestant churches. Since almost everything the Bible tells us about Mary appears in the gospel infancy narratives (the annunciation, the visitation, the virginal conception, her maternity in Bethlehem, the presentation in the Temple, the prediction of a sword piercing her heart, and the finding of Jesus in the Temple), Christmas had become a great Marian feast as well as the feast of the Nativity. But Protestants no longer treated Christmas in that way.

The Protestant focus on scriptural authenticity quickly led to an intra-Protestant debate. Could Christians do only what the Bible specified or could they do what the Bible did not specifically condemn? A similar debate had occurred thirteen centuries earlier in North Africa with conservative hardliners taking the first position and the majority of Africans taking the second. The sixteenth-century debate related directly to Christmas.

As we saw earlier, the first Christians did not celebrate Christmas. The gospels speak of Jesus' birth but make no mention of any feast in honor of that birth. The early Christians knew that, and they decided in third century North Africa that it was all right to celebrate Christmas because, even though the Bible did not mention a feast, it did not forbid the celebration of Jesus' birth.

Actually the early Christian concern about extrabiblical elements did not focus on Christmas but on issues of wider importance, such as the use of Greek philosophical terminology in Christian theology; for example, words like "person" and "nature" do not enter into New Testament presentations of Jesus. Likewise for the sixteenth-century Protestants, the real issue was what they considered the lack of explicit biblical support for many of Catholic teachings, such as the seven sacraments and the role of the papacy. Christmas was a sidelight, although in England it would become a major issue.

Martin Luther liked Christmas and saw no need to give it up. He liked it so much that he wrote Christmas hymns, such as "From Heaven Above to Earth I Come" and "To Shepherds as They Watched by Night." He also adapted a fourteenth-century hymn, "We Praise You, Lord Jesus, at Your Birth," and he translated some other hymns.

Luther preached during Advent and on Christmas and Epiphany. His sermons reflect his dual calling as scholar and pastor. They contain much learning and presume the congregation's familiarity with the scriptural narrative. One of his best and best-known sermons was one for Christmas Day on Luke 2:1-14 (the census and trip to Bethlehem).

Luther explained some of the technical questions, made reference to contemporary life ("tax collectors" in the Bible are called "notorious sinners" in German), and, this being the early stages of Reformation, compared "the pope's government" with Jesus' renunciation of earthly powers. The reformer could not pass up the chance to contrast their humility with "the glitter and gold" of Catholic churches. But the heart of the sermon lies in what Luther said to the congregants about observing Christmas.

He praised Mary, thus countering Catholic claims that Protestants attacked her devotion, but Luther focused on her hu-

mility, obedience, and the irony of her situation ("despised at
the inns although worthy to ride in state in a chariot of gold").
He compared the lowly Mary to the "wives and daughters of
prominent men at her time" about whom we now know nothing; he also pointed to the rigors of the journey in winter (he
was in Germany) and how chilly the stable must have been,
an effective touch, since he pointed out that Joseph and Mary
could not light a fire in a stable filled with flammable straw.

From Mary's humility, he moved to that of Jesus: "As much
as it [Jesus' birth] was despised on earth, so much and a thousand times more it was praised in heaven. . . . How could
God have shown his sublime goodness more than by hum-
bling himself to partake of flesh and blood?" Sensibly Luther
pointed to the importance of faith: "if someone believes this,
he can boast of the treasure that Mary is his rightful mother,
Christ his brother, and God his father." He argued that the
light that surrounded the shepherds, the heavenly light of the
angels, "is the light of the Gospel, which shines around us
from heaven through the apostles and their followers who
preach the Gospel." Pointing out that "Bethlehem" in Hebrew
means "house of bread," Luther identified the bread as the
teaching of Christ that leaves no one unsatisfied (http://www.
orlutheran.com/html/mlselk2.html).

Maintaining this allegorizing of the gospel text, he chose a
rather surprising topic, the swaddling clothes, which "are as a
rule of two kinds, the outside of coarse woolen cloth, the
inner of linen." The coarse cloth is the law of the Old Testament; the linen is the words of the prophets about Jesus. The
topic of coarse cloth leads into a discussion of the shepherds,
plain men, "despised and unknown to the world which sleeps
in the night," but to these humble folk came the first announcement of Jesus' birth (ibid.).

He also used traditional interpretative themes, such as the
New Adam and the light coming into a world of darkness.

This and his other sermons demonstrate Luther's personal
commitment to Christmas as a religious feast of great value.

In fact, so great was Luther's fondness for Christmas that a legend grew up about him as the "inventor" of the Christmas tree. As the story goes, he was going home on a clear winter evening and saw a fir tree covered by snow and with the bright stars behind it in the sky. Overcome by the beauty of the scene, he rushed home to tell his family. But he could not do so adequately, so he returned to the tree, cut it down, and brought it into his house. Naturally the snow melted quickly and the stars were outside, so Luther put candles on the tree to decorate it and to symbolize the stars with their light. This was the first Christmas tree in Germany. It is a good story, but a legend through and through.

Another legend portrayed Luther inaugurating the tradition of the *Christkind* or Christ Child as the bringer of gifts at Christmas. Supposedly it bothered Luther that gift giving had made Saint Nicholas very popular around Christmas time, and Luther wished to counter that, at least in Germany and the Protestant parts of Switzerland. Once again, a good story, but pure legend.

But if Luther favored Christmas, some other Protestants did not. Recall that debate in North Africa—these Protestants believed that Christians should only do what the Bible pre-scribes, and the Bible does not mention Christmas. Several Protestant groups thought this way, especially the Calvinists, who were entrenched in France and Switzerland but quickly spread by the middle of the sixteenth century into Germany, Eastern Europe, and Scotland. These believers refused to cele-brate Christmas.

It did not take long for Catholics to answer this attack.

Peter Canisius (1521–97) was a Jesuit priest who did mis-sionary work in Germany, trying to win back Protestant areas to Catholicism. He knew that many believers held Christmas in high regard, even if it was not mentioned in the Bible (like all Catholics, Canisius accepted officially acknowledged non-biblical ecclesiastical traditions). He opened one sermon with this response:

The Protestants are not a little surprised and scandalized at the way we Catholics celebrate the Lord's Nativity. Faithful to Christian tradition, we see nothing wrong with putting on a grand and joyous display. . . . And why not? Are we supposed to restrain our joy on the Birthday of Christ our Lord? (http://www.therealpresence.org/archives/Saints/Saints_030.htm)

Canisius went on to point out that celebrating a birthday is something natural; even pagans do it. But wanting to counter Calvinist biblical arguments, he cites Abraham's rejoicing when Sarah gave birth to Isaac, Elkanah's rejoicing when Hannah gave birth to Samuel, and Zachary and Elizabeth's rejoicing at the birth of John the Baptist. He finished the argument by asking, why can we rejoice at the births of earthly kings, but we cannot rejoice at the birth of Jesus?

But he did more than go on the attack. He insisted that Jesus fulfilled the hopes of the prophets, even going back to Adam who looked for someone of his seed to crush the head of the serpent. As we would expect, Marian devotion played a role in Canisius's understanding of Christmas; she "brought forth her child without pain." Borrowing from a homily of Augustine of Hippo, Canisius claimed Christmas as a day of universal joy. "Children should rejoice because on this day God Himself became as one of them; virgins, because a Virgin brought forth and remained unstained even after giving birth; wives, because one of their number became the Mother of God." Unfortunately he also used another tradition as old as Augustine: "Were we not to celebrate the Feast of Christmas . . . we would be worse than the stiff-necked Jews" (ibid.).

Canisius presented the traditional Catholic approach to Christmas, and, while Luther and he inevitably disagreed, they both favored the feast.

Another Christian church, neither Catholic nor Protestant, also preserved Christmas. As is well known, Henry VIII abandoned Roman Catholicism over the issue of who should head the church of England, king or pope? Henry believed that he was the head of the church, and so he left the Roman communion and established, with the help of his bishops, the Anglican Church, formally known as the Church of England. The Anglicans looked for what they called the middle way between Roman Catholicism and Protestantism. They did not accept the papacy and believed in the primacy of Scripture, but they also accepted the value of early church traditions, including the first ecumenical councils and the writings of the church fathers. To the fury of right-wing Protestants, the Anglican Church kept bishops, vestments, candles, and stained-glass windows among other "relics of popery" as the Calvinists claimed. The Anglicans also kept Christmas.

Henry VIII genuinely liked Christmas and held gigantic feasts to celebrate it. In 1514 he had a richly decorated minimountain brought into the dining hall. The mount opened and out came six beautiful, well-dressed ladies of the court to dance with the king and his lords. Henry's successors on the throne also celebrated Christmas, and the Anglican Church produced impressive Christmas ceremonies.

On Christmas Day in 1622 an Anglican bishop named Lancelot Andrewes (1555–1626) preached a sermon before King James I (1603–25). Andrewes was a great scholar who routinely included Latin phrases in his sermons, but he could get to the heart of the matter. In this sermon he focused on the magi as symbols of all believers, "their errand, our errand." Andrewes emphasized their faith, following a star from their homeland, not asking Herod and his court if the newborn King of the Jews actually existed but simply, "where is he?" In an age of great astronomers (Kepler, Galileo), Andrewes said the magi's star transcended nature, bearing a truth no celestial observation could ever discover but one known to the pagan prophet Balaam centuries before.

The scholar in Andrewes claimed to have found evidence for the star in Roman pagan writings, but the bishop rose to great heights when describing the hardships of the magi's journey "through deserts waste and desolate . . . over the rocks and crags of Arabia" on roads plied by "thieves and robbers. . . . a wearisome, irksome, troublesome, dangerous, unseasonable journey, and all this they still came." And what should the king and his attendants take away from this sermon? "There now remains nothing but to include ourselves, and bear our part with them, and with the angels, and all who this day adored Him" (http://anglicanhistory.org/lact/andrewes/v1/sermon15.html).

A Catholic contemporary of Andrewes, the Italian Jesuit Robert Bellarmine (1542–1621), also enjoyed a widespread reputation as a preacher. He had a great interest in the liturgy. He spoke of Christ's threefold birth—in heaven without a mother, on earth without a father, and then in the hearts of believers—and he contended the three masses offered on Christmas in Catholic churches corresponded to those three births. At the midnight mass, "we celebrate the human birth of Christ when, in the depths of all-pervading silence out of the middle of the night the almighty Word of God leapt down from his throne in the heavens to take up his abode among the children of men." The second mass at dawn recalled "the spiritual birth of Christ in our souls. Finally, in the full light of day, we commemorate that ineffable, everlasting birth by which the Word of God and true light is generated for all eternity from the heavenly Father of Lights" (http://www.therealpresence.org/archives/Saints/Saints_025.htm).

Naturally Catholic traditions appear in his sermon; for example, Mary endured no labor pains, her body retained its integrity, and she remained perpetually a virgin. But Bellarmine relied primarily on the Bible and ancient traditions, including the sun of righteousness and Jesus' birth at the stroke of midnight.

In a word, Christmas flourished in the sixteenth century in most of Christian Europe, yet the Calvinists would have their successes in central Europe and Scotland but perhaps most surprisingly in England.

Elizabeth I (1558–1603) reigned as head of the Church of England. She feared the Catholic powers, and rightly so as the Spanish Armada of 1588 proved. But she also wanted to keep rigorist Protestants at bay. The English rigorists technically were not Protestants and did not initially see themselves as such, but they had a strong, Calvinist-inspired desire to "purify" the Anglican Church of "popish" remnants, especially in liturgical matters and even more especially in the observation of Christmas. Their Anglican enemies gave them the name by which they have been forever known—Puritans.

The Puritans made little progress under the sharp and forceful Elizabeth. When she died childless in 1603, Parliament arranged to have her succeeded by James VI of Scotland, a descendant of Henry VII (Elizabeth's grandfather), who took the name James I of England. While in Scotland, he had come to loathe Calvinists who wanted to put religious restrictions on royal power. Once on the English throne James sided repeatedly with Anglicans and the aristocracy; the sulking Puritans countered him by building up their power in Parliament. In 1625 James died and was succeeded by his son, who reigned as Charles I (1625–49). The new king never realized how powerful religious motives were in Parliament. He had little sympathy for Calvinists, and his father had arranged a diplomatic marriage between Charles and a French princess; diplomacy aside, the Puritans saw with horror a reigning king of England with a Catholic wife. A number of governmental and financial issues estranged the king from Parliament; in 1643 the two went to war. The parliamentary army, filled with Puritans and led by the brilliant general Oliver Cromwell, defeated the royalist forces. Parliament tried the captured king for high treason and in 1649 executed him. England had gone from a monarchy to a commonwealth.

Dominant in Parliament, the triumphant Puritans now set out to make England "a godly state," that is, a country reflecting Puritan values. The process reached into every corner, but opposition to Christmas was a centerpiece.

The Puritans objected to the day itself because it had no scriptural foundation, and they also objected to how it was celebrated, that is, the heavy eating and drinking, dancing, card-playing, and masquerades. In the 1580s a Puritan named Philip Stubbs complained "that more mischief is that time committed than in all the year besides, what masking and mumming, whereby robbery, whoredom, murder (!?) and whatnot is committed" (Durston, 8).

But given the day's popularity, the parliamentary Puritans had to move carefully. In 1643, at Puritan urging, some shopkeepers kept their stores open on December 25, that is, they did not treat Christmas as a holiday. This irreverence outraged the population, and some young men actually attacked the shops. In 1644 Christmas fell on the last Wednesday of the month, a day on which the Puritans usually fasted. Parliament declared December 25 to be a fast day and one to be observed more stringently than usual to make up for reveling that some people would inevitably do. Parliament met and did business on that day.

Gaining confidence, Parliament in 1647 legally abolished the feast of Christmas (along with Easter). When some Anglican priests put up decorations, the police arrested them. Bravely, they held Christmas services in prison. Parliament increased the penalties and pressure, in 1652 ordering shops to be kept open on Christmas. People who celebrated Christmas were thought to be royalists who were disloyal to Parliament or possibly even Catholics preserving "papist" ways.

The Puritans living in New England felt the same way. But the North American colonies like Plymouth and Massachusetts hesitated to outlaw Christmas, not doing it until 1659. They did not, however, arrest anyone for celebrating the day but rather established a fine of five shillings.

But the British populace came to loathe the oppressive Puritan government, and in 1660 Charles II, son of the executed king, returned to Britain. He promptly restored the celebration along with numerous other things outlawed by the Puritans.

The New England Puritans continued to outlaw Christmas until 1681, when their colonies came under royal rule and received an Anglican governor.

Although the Puritans failed to eradicate Christmas, they had succeeded in both England and North America in raising questions about the appropriateness of the feast and the way it was celebrated. They not only proved that December 25 had no scriptural warrant but they also contended that Christmas was just a papal Christianizing of the pagan Roman feast of Saturnalia. How could such a day honor Christ's birth?

Nor were the Puritans the only ones with doubts about the holidays. The Quakers, founded by George Fox (1624–91), believed in religious freedom for all and would not try to prevent anyone else's form of worship, but they refused to celebrate Christmas, proof that not only Calvinists and Puritans had doubts about it.

While most Britons continued to celebrate Christmas joyfully, they could not escape Puritan arguments about whether true Christians should celebrate Christ's birthday with *such* raucous practices. While the monarchs and aristocrats continued to celebrate elaborate Christmas parties, more and more families in Britain and North America toned down the celebrations.

But we cannot leave the English Puritans without looking at the poem "On the Morning of Christ's Nativity," composed in 1629 by the greatest of Puritan poets, John Milton (1608–74). This poem demonstrates that no matter how much Puritans might loathe Christmas, they appreciated the Nativity. Milton invoked a number of traditional themes:

> To sit the midst of Trinal Unity,
> He laid aside, and, here with us to be,
>   Forsook the courts of everlasting day,
> And chose with us a darksome house of mortal clay.

. . . .

It was the winter wild,
While the heaven-born child
All meanly wrapt in the rude manger lies;
Nature, in awe to him,
Had doffed her gaudy trim,

. . . .

No war, or battle's sound,
Was heard the world around;
The idle spear and shield were high uphung;
The hooked chariot stood,
Unstained with hostile blood;

. . . .

But peaceful was the night
Wherein the Prince of Light
His reign of peace upon the earth began.
The winds, with wonder whist,
Smoothly the waters kissed,
Whispering new joys to the mild Ocean,
Who now hath quite forgot to rave,
While birds of calm sit brooding on the charmed wave.

The Puritan poet included far more than what the Bible says
about Jesus' birth, but he could do so because he was writing
poetry, not theology. Perhaps reflecting the building tension in
England between Parliament and the throne, Milton emphasized the traditional theme of universal peace in the natural
world and even among humans. Theologically he spoke of the
Son of God leaving heaven to humble himself as one of us. It
is a traditional theme, to be sure, but has anyone else ever expressed it so well?

Although we will focus on Christmas in English-speaking
lands, we must remember that in most of Catholic Europe
and in Lutheran areas, no one questioned the importance of
Christmas, which continued with liturgical ceremonies that
horrified its Calvinist critics.

By the seventeenth century we are in the Baroque period, when music featured not only instruments of all kinds but also growing choirs of both men and women as well as soloists for whom composers wrote special parts. This practice was shunned by Medieval monks for whom humble anonymity was required. Free from Medieval restraints, Catholic composers ranged widely, starting in the Renaissance.

The great Giovanni Pierluigi Palestrina (1525–94) brought Catholic liturgical music to new heights, reflecting the desires of the popes that the church take advantage of new cultural developments. His 1575 mass, *Hodie Christus natus est* ("Today Christ Has Been Born"), remains a masterpiece of the genre. Spain, the leader of Catholic Europe in this period, produced Tomás Luis de Victoria (1548–1611), who wrote several pieces for Christmas, the most often played being *O Magnum Mysterium* ("O Great Mystery"). Probably the best-known piece is Arcangelo Corelli's (1653–1713) concerto grosso number 8, popularly known as the Christmas concerto, a piece widely played today.

Protestant composers also wrote on Christmas, and two Lutherans, among the greatest composers who ever lived, have left monuments to Christmas. Both were born in the second half of the seventeenth century, right after the English Puritans had lost their power but still exercised influence. Johann Sebastian Bach (1685–1750) was a devout Lutheran who had a lifelong association with his church, from a chorister as a boy, a composer of ecclesiastical music (he wrote secular music as well), and organist and composer at Saint Thomas Church, Leipzig, from 1723 until his death; he also composed pieces for another Leipzig church, Saint Nicholas. In an age often marred by religious friction, Bach accepted a commission to write his great *Mass in B Minor*, the first parts of which he presented to the Catholic king of Poland. His six-part masterpiece, the Christmas oratorio, was composed for Christmas 1734, although he added to it later. No matter what Calvinists thought, many Protestants rejoiced in music for the Nativity.

George Friedrich Handel (1685–1759), another German Lutheran, studied with a church organist and at one point was *Kapellmeister* (chapel master of music) for George, elector of Hanover, a Protestant state. When the Stuart dynasty of England expired in 1714 with the death of Queen Anne, Parliament searched for a Protestant monarch, eventually turning to a great-grandson of King James I. That man was the elector George of Hanover, who became King George I of England (1714–27). Before his former patron became king, Handel had been working in England for some time. He had composed music for Queen Anne, who gave him a pension, which his former and now royal patron increased. Handel soon decided to stay in England, where he composed a number of religious pieces but especially oratorios, in which choirs and soloists retold biblical stories. The libretto for his most famous work, *Messiah*, dealt mostly with Christ's suffering and resurrection. Handel wrote it in 1741, and it premiered in Dublin on April 13, 1742. It was not written as a Christmas piece, although it—or rather its *Hallelujah* chorus—has become *the* Christmas concert work.

The period from the Reformation to the eighteenth century also offers us some well-known songs, such as "Joseph dearest, Joseph mine," from an anonymous text dating to the late Middle Ages but the hymn as we have it is from a Catholic hymnal of 1605 in Mainz, Germany. In this tender piece, one of the few to even notice Joseph, Mary asks her husband to rock the child Jesus. A German hymn, *Wachet auf* ("Awake, Awake"), was written by Philipp Nicolai (1556–1608), a Lutheran pastor. Bach later wrote the music for it, which is how we know it today.

The end of this period saw the Latin composition of *Adeste, Fideles* by an English Catholic, John Francis Wade (1711–86), who taught at the English College in Douai, France, at a time when Catholics were not welcome in British universities. By 1789 an anonymous translator had turned it into "Come, faithful all." In 1841 Francis Oakley, an Anglican priest, produced the best-known translation, "O Come, All Ye Faithful." In 1719, an English Protestant pastor, Isaac Watts (1674–1748), gave us "Joy to the World."

The visual arts also changed in this period. Many Renaissance artists paid attention to the historical circumstances of Jesus' birth, and they portrayed Mary and Joseph as poor people. One could still find regal portraits of Virgin and Child, but for Nativity paintings Mary remained a peasant, although rarely a Jewish one. Artists routinely gave her European features, especially northern ones such as blue eyes and light-colored hair. The list of Italian Catholics portraying the Nativity includes the greatest names, such as da Vinci, Michelangelo, and Raphael, but also a host of lesser-known artists.

Although Calvinists had difficulty with religious art, other Protestants did not. The German Lutheran Albrecht Dürer (1471–1528) did several magnificent Nativity scenes. The Dutch painter Pieter Bruegel the Elder (1525–69) portrayed "The Slaughter of the Holy Innocents" by setting it in contemporary Holland during an attack on a village by the occupying Spaniards. This dramatic work includes two Spanish officers, seated on horseback, chatting and joking while Dutch parents fruitlessly implore their mercy on the children. Less dramatically, Bruegel portrayed the arrival of the magi in the middle of a northern European winter. In the next generation, another Dutchman, Rembrandt van Rijn (1606–69), would paint haunting nativities with a superb use of light and color.

This period also produced the first unquestionable work of Christmas art, that is, art not of the Nativity but of Christmas itself. Bruegel showed winter scenes at Christmas, including ice skaters. But particularly important are paintings of "The Bean King." In northern European Christmas celebrations, including English ones, the host would put a bean into a cake and then bake it. The person whose piece of cake included the bean would be the king for the evening. The Flem-

ish painter Jacob Jordaens (1593–1678) portrayed a
Christmas party at which an elderly man wearing a paper
crown drinks down a glass of wine while others who have also
been drinking stand around, cheering him on. Significantly,
no child can be found in this picture. Another Jordaens paint-
ing on a similar theme does show a child—an infant resting
in his mother's right arm while she toasts the bean king with
a glass of wine in her left hand! The secular Christmas had
arrived in art.

We also find Christmas poems focusing on the secular celebration of the day. The English poet Robert Herrick (1591–
1674) was an Anglican priest and vicar who wrote a great deal
of Christmas religious poetry, much of it very moving, so his
vigorous, joyful poems about the secular side of Christmas do
not reflect any disparagement or disinterest in the religious
side. Herrick clearly believed the two could go hand in hand.
Here are excerpts from his "Ceremonies for Christmas":

> Come, bring with a noise,
> My merry, merry boys
> The Christmas log to the firing;
> While my good dame, she
> Bids ye all be free,
> And drink to your hearts' desiring.

> With the last year's brand
> Light the new block, and
> For good success in his spending
> On your psaltries play,
> That sweet luck may
> Come while the log is a-tending.
> Drink now the strong beer,
> Cut the white loaf here;
> The while the meat is a-shredding
> For the rare mince-pie,
> And the plums stand by
> To fill the paste that's a-kneading.

The religious Christmas flourished in Catholic countries, in several Protestant ones, and in England with a religiously mixed population, but the secular Christmas was growing quickly. In the nineteenth century, especially in Great Britain and the United States, the secular celebration would challenge the traditional secular/religious balance, and it would even modify the religious one, especially in urban areas. Let us try simultaneously to keep an eye on Britain as we head across the Atlantic to America.

CHAPTER SIX

The Rise of the Secular Christmas

In the nineteenth century, Great Britain and the United States created the modern secular Christmas. Thanks to the astonishing reach of contemporary communications media, this Anglo-American version has spread throughout the world, impacting virtually every country that celebrates the day.

The first English settlers in North America arrived at Roanoke Island in the colony of Virginia (now part of North Carolina) in 1585; the colony foundered, and the colonists returned home. Another colony was founded there in 1587 but "the Lost Colony" literally disappeared from the face of the earth. Jamestown, founded in 1607 and also in Virginia, became the first permanent English settlement in North America, but we have no information on if or how any of these groups celebrated Christmas. Ironically, the first notice of Christmas in English America comes from the Puritans who hated the holiday.

A Puritan group, commonly known in the United States as the Pilgrims, arrived in Plymouth in modern Massachusetts in 1620. They made Plymouth a Puritan colony, but ships coming from England inevitably included some non-Puritans among their crews and passengers. On Christmas Day, 1621, a group of these non-Puritans told the Pilgrim governor William Bradford that it was "against their conscience" to work on Christmas Day. Bradford accommodated them and let them off from work to celebrate a religious holiday. But later in the day he discovered a number of them engaged in sports, that is, they were enjoying the secular side of Christmas. The infuriated governor told the young men involved that it was against his conscience for them to play on a day they claimed was sacred and ordered them to stop playing and to observe Christmas in a religious fashion.

But when the Puritans fell from power in England in 1660, the new king, Charles II, had little use for Puritan colonies in North America. In 1681 Massachusetts Bay and Plymouth colonies fell under royal control, which meant a royal governor in Boston, and that governor was an Anglican. Naturally he wanted to celebrate Christmas, and in 1686 he had to walk to a religious service with a bodyguard as angry Puritans shouted at him. But by the early eighteenth century even the Puritans had come to accept the existence of Christmas, even if they did not observe it. The influential Puritan theologian Cotton Mather opposed Christmas because it had no scriptural warrant, but he said he could tolerate it if people celebrated it as a religious holiday and did not engage in raucous behavior.

Scotch-Irish Calvinist immigrants in the eighteenth century increased the number of those who loathed the Anglican Church and refused to celebrate Christmas. These newcomers settled in a number of colonies.

But the middle (New York, New Jersey, Delaware) and southern (Virginia, North and South Carolina, Georgia) colonies had many Anglicans who did celebrate Christmas. Joining them were the Dutch Reformed Christians in New York, German Lutherans and Catholics who had settled in religiously free Pennsylvania, Catholics in Maryland, and German Moravians who settled in Pennsylvania and then migrated to North Carolina. Joining the Puritans were other Calvinist groups such as Presbyterians and Baptists; the Quakers in Pennsylvania also declined to celebrate Christmas.

Elements of the secular Christmas appeared early. German Lutherans brought the decorated Christmas tree with them;

the Moravians put lighted candles on those trees. The Pennsylvania Germans also had the *Christkind* or Christ Child who brought gifts on December 24. (This German word later metamorphosed into Kris Kringle.) English settlers brought holly, ivy, mistletoe, carols (secular and religious), and a notion of general festivity. The colonists did not, however, emphasize gift giving. When people did exchange presents, it was often on New Year's Day, while the Dutch Reformed, although Protestants, preferred their traditional custom of giving gifts on Saint Nicholas Day. Most celebrations had music; in the southern colonies people lighted firecrackers and shot off guns.

Practices differed from colony to colony, church to church, ethnic group to ethnic group, and people generally accepted this status quo. But, when the Revolution succeeded and the United States became a reality in 1783, the situation changed.

The new country contained a great many poor people who came in hope of a better life, and who settled in the eastern cities, especially New York. This situation concerned a group of wealthy, educated New York men, who recognized that two very distinct social groups were forming. This group believed that the people in the lower socioeconomic group—they would have said "lower class"—would profit best by following their economic and social "betters," but they struggled to find a way to bridge this gap and convince the poor to do so. One member of that group, the writer Washington Irving (1783–1859), thought Christmas could help.

Although not overly wealthy (he worked all his life), Irving was well connected, being good friends with Martin Van Buren, the eighth president of the United States, among others. Worried about the rich-poor gap, Irving recalled that in England the aristocracy traditionally invited the people who worked their lands to come to the big house on Christmas Day, temporarily bridging the social breach, although only with poor people known to the rich. Irving did not expect to replicate that in the United States, and he also knew that this tradition was fading in England, but he believed that if people knew about the joy spread by a traditional English Christmas with mixed social groups, they might see a way to bridge the gap between classes.

In 1819 he published *The Sketch Book*, a collection of essays and stories, including his two most famous works, "Rip Van Winkle" and "The Legend of Sleepy Hollow." It also included five chapters about Christmas in a traditional English country house belonging to the fictional Bracebridge family. Irving gave lip service to the religious nature of the day, referring once to "our Savior's birth," and when the Bracebridge family went to church, they endured a boring sermon and rejoiced when the service ended. For Irving, the real joy of Christmas lay with a family reunion, being in a warm house on a cold day with lots of eating and drinking, dancing and game playing, and shared good fellowship. This joy was shared with the family's landed tenants. Irving wondered if and hoped that the spirit of Christmas might bring Americans together, even for a little while. Those hopes did not materialize. Rural British aristocrats may have invited poor people they knew to the big house, but wealthy Americans increasingly separated themselves from the poor. There were literally no poor people whom the rich would and could invite to their homes. The class gap continued to grow in the United States. Yet Irving's account of Bracebridge Hall did change Christmas in both Great Britain and the United States with his portrayal of the joyous secular celebration. Indeed, for many people it became a model. (For some it still is. Every year the Alwahnee Hotel at Yosemite National Park sponsors the Bracebridge Dinner.)

Irving did not criticize the religious feast, but when the best-selling author in the United States and first American to be a best seller in Great Britain focused on the joys of a secular Christmas, people paid attention. To an extent, Irving succeeded in advocating a holiday that all Americans would celebrate, but he also created the first of the three great literary building blocks of the secular Christmas.

Three years later, in 1822, came the second one when another prominent New Yorker, Clement Clarke Moore (1779–1863), wrote a poem for his children entitled "A Visit from Saint Nicholas," more popularly known as "The Night before Christmas." A biblical scholar and son of an Episcopal bishop, Moore had great appreciation of the religious Christmas. Yet his poem deals with a secular event, the visit to his home by the old Dutch version of Saint Nicholas who drives a sled pulled by eight reindeer and gives gifts to children.

He took material about the saint from Washington Irving's 1809 fictional history, *A Knickerbocker's History of New York*. Moore also apparently borrowed some of it from an anonymous poem that appeared in 1821 in a children's magazine named *The Children's Friend*. The poem spoke of Santeclause delivering gifts to children on Christmas Eve. But Moore's poem surpassed both of these in popularity when, in 1823 a newspaper in Troy, New York, published the poem anonymously, supposedly having gotten it from a woman who had visited Moore's home and copied it out. It became immensely popular nationwide and probably a bit embarrassing to a man known as a biblical scholar; not until 1844 did he acknowledge his authorship.

The poem changed Christmas in the United States and other countries as well. Moore identified the gift giver as Saint Nicholas, who traditionally brought gifts on December 5, the eve of his feast day, but Moore transferred the day to Christmas Eve. As the poem became popular, Christmas overshadowed Saint Nicholas Day as a day to give gifts; it also gradually eliminated New Year's as the day for that practice. Although Moore had nothing to do with it, the saint subsequently changed too, becoming Santa (= Saint) Claus (dropping the first syllable of Nicholas). The poem makes no mention of gifts to adults, only children, and Christmas was on its way to being *the* children's holiday.

In 1843 the third building block of the secular Christmas appeared. Charles Dickens published a novella entitled *A*

Christmas Carol. It barely mentions the religious nature of the feast; the supernatural figures in the story are not angels but ghosts. The story also downplays the redemptive role once given to Christ's birth; now the ghosts redeem Scrooge from his cold-blooded obsession with money. "He went to church" is literally all that Dickens says about Scrooge's religious observation of the feast. But the author does emphasize the fellowship shared all over Britain on Christmas—poor miners who have little else but have joy on Christmas; two lighthouse keepers, alone and isolated, share a pint of grog at midnight; and, of course, the Cratchits and Scrooge's nephew Fred and his wife all enjoy the day.

This novella turned out to be Dickens's most popular work, partly because he wrote it during the Industrial Revolution, when loathsome working conditions, far worse than those Bob Cratchit endured, oppressed laboring people in Great Britain and the United States. Dickens claimed that the Christmas spirit of generosity could ameliorate at least some of this suffering.

These three works do not attack the religious feast; they simply say little or nothing about it. On the other hand, they emphasize values that Christians could agree with. All stress the importance of the family, especially Dickens, who shows how Scrooge has cut himself off from familial love, and Irving, who virtually equates family and Christmas. The three authors also stress the positive elements of gift giving, and for Irving and Dickens, the meals and the parties serve to bring people together. Yet they did weaken the religious aspect of the holiday by placing the family celebration ahead of it.

Moore intended to write a delightful poem for his children, but the other two authors set out to make Christmas, as they understood it to be, a major holiday. Now the central element of Christmas was not Christ's birth but a family get-together. These two do not essentially conflict, but a family get-together could easily be held with no religious overtones at all. To be sure, many people simply celebrate both, going to

church and being with their families, but the absolute link of
Christ with Christmas had been broken.

But as the secular holiday grew, the religious feast continued to move people in the nineteenth century, sometimes in
public ways. Churches and other Christian groups, such as
the Salvation Army founded by Catherine and William Booth
in London in 1865, urged people to celebrate Christmas by
imitating Christ, who was born in a lowly stable and whose
first visitors were poor shepherds, by helping the impoverished and the suffering. Working on the now popular theme
of Christmas as a family holiday, Christian leaders reminded
people that we all belong to God's family, many of whose
members need their brothers' and sisters' aid and comfort. In
a word, the churches succeeded, turning Christmas into the
major season for charitable giving.

The religious Christmas also survived in many small ways
as individuals made life happier for others at that time. Some
of the best examples of this come from the American frontier,
where Christian warmth helped people in even the harshest
of winters, and these examples show how the religious elements can persist even when the secular element is there.
They even show how the two can compliment one another.

In the 1850s in the new state of Iowa, churches held fairs
and suppers at Christmas to raise money for charity, especially to help farmers who were struggling. Sometimes the
fairs were enhanced by a visit from a Methodist circuit rider,
that is, a minister who went from town to town and church
to church, regardless of the weather—one of the true heroes
of Christianity on the frontier. In Kansas, German settlers
and refugees from czarist persecution in Russia brought their
Christkind with them and showed the appreciative Americans
their religious Christmas.

The goldfields of Montana received immigrants from Eastern Europe coming to make their (hoped-for) fortunes. Many
were Orthodox Christians who celebrated Christmas on

January 7, and thus Christmas Eve fell on January 6. Slavic settlers in Butte explained to the locals that, in their tradition, the first visitor to a home at midnight on Christmas Eve should scatter wheat on the family members, a symbol of a good harvest, and say the words "Christ is born," to which the family members would reply, "Truly, he is born," and then scatter wheat upon their visitor.

A Belgian Jesuit, Pierre Jean De Smet, worked among the native tribes of the Pacific Northwest. He gave an account of midnight mass in 1844 when the Native Americans came to his small wooden church and fired their guns to announce the birth of Jesus. They then sang a hymn in De Smet's native French. De Smet emphasized that his church had elaborate decorations, as Catholic churches do at Christmas, but the decorations were often fashioned from the trees and plants that grew locally. "A grand banquet, according to Indian custom, followed the first Mass. . . . the whole assembly might be compared to the *agape* of the first Christians" (Baur, 211).

Both cattle ranchers and sheepherders settled in the Wyoming territory, and often friction arose between them. A Wyoming cattleman's wife, Elinor Stewart, learned that some local sheepherders had little to eat at Christmas. Keeping her project secret from the cattlemen, she arranged for butter, jam, and meat to be sent to the sheepherding families, "perhaps remembering who were the Christ Child's first visitors" (Baur, 253).

An Episcopal priest, Cyrus Townsend Brady, worked on the Great Plains in Nebraska and Kansas. One Christmas morning he left home for a long buggy ride to a cold and drafty church. Brady conducted the service in a fur cap and buffalo-skin coat. His poor parishioners insisted he join them for a Christmas meal. They had so little to eat that Brady contributed to the dinner with a mince pie that his wife had given him for a Christmas present. Brady received a greater present when a little girl told him, "The pie makes it seem like Christmas after all" (Baur 263). Moved by this, he hustled back to his church, took the collection basket, tied some ribbons on it, gave his host family the money, and gave their children the gifts that his own children had given to him. This wonderful man Christianized the secular element of Christmas.

Throughout the nineteenth century the religious opposition to Christmas was diminishing, partly because those who opposed it steadily became a smaller proportion of the American population. German immigrants had been coming to North America for well over a century, but immigration from German lands increased in the 1820s. These immigrants were Lutherans or Catholics, which meant that they celebrated Christmas. As they radiated out from the traditional German-American bases in Pennsylvania and North Carolina, they brought Christmas with them.

But German immigration was soon overwhelmed by massive immigration from Ireland. Immigrants from the Emerald Isle had been coming to British North America for some time. Initially, most were Calvinist Protestants from northern Ireland, but the devastating potato crop failure and ensuing famine (1846–49) sent more than two million Irish to America, with smaller groups going to Canada. Almost all were Catholics who, of course, celebrated Christmas, although for some time they had precious little to celebrate and precious little to celebrate with. By 1860 Roman Catholicism had become the country's largest religious group, and its growth had just begun. In the second half of the nineteenth century immigrants came from Hungary, Italy, and Poland, swelling the Catholic total. By the end of the century more than one in five Americans were Catholic. When they were added to the many Protestants who observed the feast, a sizeable majority of Americans celebrated Christmas.

Although Catholics enlarged the numbers of celebrants, simultaneously increasing numbers of American Protestants came to question the rigid, uncompromising Calvinism inherited from the Puritans. But they could not question just things like predestination; slowly but surely they questioned other aspects of Calvinism, such as its rejection of Christmas. As we have seen, Calvinists opposed Christmas because it is not in the Bible, December 25 cannot be proven to be the date of Christ's birth, and the celebration of the day was often raucous. When Christmas started to become a day for children, some Calvinists argued further against it on the grounds that children, born steeped in the guilt of original sin, were sinners who did not deserve such a holiday. To the children's rescue came a new religious group, the Unitarians, who denied original sin and insisted that children were born pure and innocent until adults corrupted them and that they deserved Christmas. The Unitarians simply made a full-scale, successful attack on Calvinist attitudes toward children.

The secular Christmas also weighed heavily upon the opponents of the religious one. As the holiday spread, Calvinist children saw other Christian children enjoying a wonderful family holiday with trees, lights, and, of course, gifts. Naturally they wondered why they were left out. Increasingly adults felt the same way. The poet Henry Wadsworth Longfellow (1807–82), a lifelong New Englander, could not totally shake off the inherited regional traditions, but he knew they were dying. In 1856 he observed, "The old Puritan feeling prevents it [Christmas] from being a cheerful, hearty holiday, though every year makes it more so" (Restad, 96). The poet was right. By 1900 most New England churches celebrated Christmas.

In 1837 the state of Louisiana, with a sizeable Catholic population from its French founding, made Christmas a legal holiday; fourteen more states did so by 1860. In 1870 Congress made it a national holiday. The opponents of Christmas retreated to their own enclaves.

The secular Christmas also furthered the religious Christmas in a strange way. In the early nineteenth century most people lived on farms, but the Industrial Revolution lured many of them, especially young men, into the factories of the growing industrial cities. At this period there were no "Christmas vacations," and people often had to work on December 24 and 26, and sometimes on the feast itself, so they could not get home and be with their families. To this can be added the many people in the United States who left their homes in the East and Midwest for land in frontier territories or for gold and silver in California, Nevada, and Montana; they might never see their loved ones again. A problem had arisen, and inevitably a solution arose.

In 1843 an Englishman produced the first Christmas card, modeled after a gentleman's calling card to be left at a home when the resident was not there. Paper manufacturers quickly recognized the potential for such cards, and they promoted the practice. It caught on in Great Britain and the United States, and rightly so since people at least wanted to send greetings to their families. The Christmas card soon became essential for those who could not be home for the holiday; it then expanded into something for people to send to all their relatives and friends, and then to business or work associates.

The earliest cards were simple greetings, but manufacturers soon put on decorations, often overly sentimental. Realizing that many people in both Britain and the United States were either illiterate or had a limited education and did not feel comfortable writing, the manufacturers added sentiments so that all anyone had to do was sign the cards. This worked well for many people, but educated, wealthy people wanted cards that would express their cultivation and breeding. Those who aped the manners of the upper class soon agreed. For the manufacturers, this was a market not to be missed.

It was possible to hire respected artists to make more sophisticated cards, but a cheaper, easier, and more suitable solution lay to hand: reproducing the art of the Great Masters, the Renaissance and Baroque painters whose works filled the country's foremost museums. But here was the catch: the Great Masters had not painted Santa Claus or country houses in winter or people dashing through the snow on a one-horse open sleigh. They painted Nativity scenes with the Holy Family, the shepherds, and the wise men. Since many of the artists, especially the French, Italians, and Spaniards, were Catholics, their paintings often emphasized the role of Mary. But they were the Great Masters, and onto the Christmas cards went their religious works.

Soon people had elegant Christmas cards (often given in lieu of gifts) that reminded them of why there was a Christmas in the first place. Eventually great nineteenth-century painters produced not only Nativity scenes but also ones reflecting the secular celebration. Yet to this day many better cards picture Christ's birth, even more so now that Medieval manuscript Nativity scenes, almost all produced in monasteries or cathedrals, have joined the Great Masters.

Museum directors eventually realized what an opportunity they had, and they licensed reproductions or printed their own cards. Now Christmas cards with superb Nativity images fill every museum store in the months before the holiday.

The nineteenth century also witnessed the creation of some of the most beautiful and popular religious Christmas music ever written. Indeed, in this area the religious Christmas has completely triumphed over the secular one. While good secular songs exist ("White Christmas," "Silver Bells"), none has approached the beauty of the religious ones, especially the ones people got to know in the nineteenth century.

An anonymous American composed "Away in a Manger" no later than 1880. An eighteenth-century Welsh New Year carol was translated anonymously into English in 1881 as "Deck the Halls with Boughs of Holly." A hymn that is immensely popular in England but largely unknown in the United States, "Once in Royal David's City," was composed by Cecil Frances Alexander in 1848. This piece is commonly sung by boys' choirs, a fitting memorial to Mrs. Alexander, who wrote didactic songs for children.

Edmund Sears, an American and descendant of the early Puritans, wrote "It Came Upon a Midnight Clear" in 1849. The Englishman John Mason Neale, a translator of Medieval and Renaissance Latin Christmas music, composed works of his own, such as "Good Christian Men Rejoice" and "Good King Wenceslas" in the 1850s. John Henry Hopkins, an Episcopal priest in Pennsylvania, wrote "We Three Kings" in 1857. Eight years later it appeared in his book *Carols, Hymns, and Songs*; five years later it was included in a British anthology.

The charming English folk song "Greensleeves" dates to at least the seventeenth century and probably the sixteenth. Around 1865, William Chatterton Dix, manager of a Scottish marine insurance company and fervent hymn writer, penned the lyrics of "What Child Is This" to the traditional melody. Today this subtle, beautiful hymn enjoys more popularity in the United States than in its home country.

An American Protestant pastor, Phillips Brooks, wrote "O Little Town of Bethlehem" in 1868, a few years after he had returned from a trip to the Holy Land. Lewis Redner, an organist at the Philadelphia church where Brooks presided, wrote the familiar tune. The English Catholic poet Christina Rossetti wrote "In the Bleak Midwinter" sometime before 1872; the current tune that popularized it was composed by Gustav Holst by 1906.

These pieces were all composed in English. The nineteenth century also saw the translation of several hymns into English. "Angels We Have Heard on High" was a traditional French carol; an English Catholic bishop named James Chadwick translated it sometime before 1860.

A fifteenth-century German carol was translated by an American, Theodore Baker, into "Lo, How E'er a Rose Is Blooming" toward the end of the century. In 1851 John Mason Neale turned *Veni, Veni, Emmanuel* into the very beautiful "O Come, O Come, Emmanuel."

A French poet named Placide Cappeau de Roquemaure wrote a poem entitled *Minuit, chrétiens*, for which Adolphe

Adam, composer of the famous ballet "Giselle," wrote some music, and the song became known in France as *Cantique de Noel*. It became popular in the United States as "O Holy Night" when a Unitarian minister, John Dwight, translated it into English in 1855.

Translation also gave the English-speaking world "Silent Night," which has been translated into 230 languages and reigns as the world's best-known and probably best-loved Christmas hymn. An Austrian priest named Joseph Mohr wrote the words, and a church organist named Franz Gruber wrote the music. They "premiered" their work at mass in the Alpine village of Oberndorf in 1818 with the title *Stille Nacht*. Copyright laws were not always followed in Austria at that time, and the Strasser family, a group of traveling minstrels (think *The Sound of Music*), used the song in their Christmas program. When they performed it at a well-publicized concert in the German city of Leipzig in 1832,they gave no credit to either Mohr or Gruber, who, when they learned what was happening, used legal means to get their authorship recognized. In 1858 Emily Elliott translated the work for the choir of Saint Mark's Church in Brighton. The song became popular on both sides of the Atlantic. An American Episcopal bishop, John Freeman Young (1820–85), produced the widely used version in a rather free translation.

Of course, by this time composers were also producing secular Christmas songs, such as James Pierpont's "Jingle Bells" (1857), but the religious pieces easily eclipsed the secular ones. (Who can name a nineteenth-century secular song besides "Jingle Bells"?)

Christian writers produced poems and even plays in the nineteenth century, and many wrote pieces about the Nativity, but they did not produce great works dealing with it, another sign that the religious Christmas was losing its previous prominence.

The rise of the secular Christmas dominates the history of the feast in the nineteenth century, but, as we have seen, the secular had always existed. The nineteenth century expanded it in size and in direction. Decorated trees, previously used only by German immigrants, became universally popular. In 1856 President Franklin Pierce had one in the White House. When the Edison Company invented electric Christmas lights so that people did not have to use open-flame candles, trees gained in popularity.

Sending cards became a universal practice; every year the Post Office reported a larger and larger volume of cards. Manufacturers modernized production. A German immigrant named Louis Prang made cards that were works of art. Not until the rise of internet e-cards did the sending of cards experience a decrease.

Since people were decorating their homes with greens, they soon augmented their celebration with a variety of other decorations and items, such as Christmas candles, china, and linen. The religious Christmas also flourished and even grew, thanks to immigration and the weakening of religious resistance to it, but the clear story of the nineteenth century is how secularized Christmas became. Yet this did not happen because of any conflict between secular and religious. Many of the retailers who advanced the secular Christmas were themselves personally religious. People who bought presents and put up trees also went to church. But a change had been made. Gift shopping took up time and energy; so did putting up decorations. The secular Christmas was solid, visible, impossible to avoid; the religious Christmas was quiet, thoughtful, and easy to put aside—but only temporarily—when the secular holiday made its demands.

Here is a striking but generally positive proof of this impact of this new secular Christmas: the turning of a religious practice into a secular one.

In the middle of the nineteenth century Irish immigrants came to the United States in enormous numbers, bringing many folk traditions with them, such as carving scary faces

into turnips at Halloween, the precursor of the jack-o'-lantern
when the immigrants used the pumpkins available in their
new home.

The Irish knew well the gospel story of the Holy Family's
search for a place to stay, and over the centuries they also had
heard amplifications of the account that had the Holy Family
being turned down multiple times by cruel landlords and
being left outside on a cold winter's night. By the nineteenth
century the Irish had created the pious and touching Christmas custom of putting candles in their windows, symbolically
offering a welcoming light to the Holy Family in their search
for a place to stay.

The immigrants to America maintained the custom, and
this appealed to other Americans, who also began to put
lights in windows. The immigrant tradition of symbolically
lighting the way for the Holy Family has, of course, long
faded, but Christmas lights continue to brighten the land-
scape during the longest days of the year. A fine religious tradition has metamorphosed into a fine secular one.

But we have now come to a turning point. The secular
Christmas has established itself, and much of it is good. So why
do so many religious people today see it as such a problem?

Two reasons. First, there is the secular Christmas in itself
(trees, lights, wreaths, gifts, dinners), and then there is what
people do with it. Some people lack a sense of balance, and in
the modern era many simply overdo the secular element,
threatening to denigrate the religious one. For example, the
transformation of the religious candles in the window into
the secular lights shows how a religious tradition might fade
but have a positive secular successor. But then comes the ex-
cess. Lights in the window become lights all over the exterior
of the house, which then become lights all over the roof, the
garage, the fence, and any other available space. And not just
lights, but lights that move, flash on and off, change color and
shape, and often do so accompanied by blaring music lest

anyone in the neighborhood miss the display. I strongly support people's right to decorate their houses as they like, but we can also see how this overwhelming megawatt display has gone a long way from the traditional secular family Christmas of the nineteenth century and can easily turn into display for the sake of display. Such an approach has become so common in Richmond, Virginia, that the city actually offers visitors a "Tacky Light Tour" of the most extensive, expensive, and tacky lighted houses in the area.

Moderation of the secular might alleviate the concerns of many religious people that the secular Christmas is an enemy of the religious one.

The second reason for concern is, I believe, far more problematic, and that is consumer*ism*. I highlight *ism* because this is a value system that teaches that possessions matter most. Consumer*ism* means the belief that getting more and more is a legitimate goal and that we measure our success in life by what we own. "My family is better than yours because we live in a bigger house and drive more expensive cars and take more luxurious vacations." Consumerism pushes us to buy the newest toys for adults; if we do not, our neighbors will notice, and then what will they think of us?

No religious person can accept consumerism. For example, if we measure people by their possessions, then the poor, a special concern of Jesus, never have any value. And if they have no value, who cares what they think? We can learn nothing from them; government, schools, industry have no need to pay attention to them. The Beatitudes may have called the poor blessed, but a consumerist value system simply dismisses them.

This repulsive, anti-Christian attitude weighs most heavily on the poor at Christmas when so much in a consumerist society insists that Christmas happiness revolves around expensive gifts, which, of course, the poor cannot afford.

Consumerism may technically be a secular phenomenon, but it has taken us a long way from the traditional secular Christmas which emphasized the family celebration, something religious people could appreciate and value. Consumerism, not the trees, lights, and cards, has become the real enemy of the religious Christmas.

To be sure, the traditional secular Christmas started us down this path, insisting that Christmas required food and drink to be bought, trees and ornaments to be bought, presents to be bought, cards and stamps to be bought, and so much else. There had been nothing like this before in the history of Christmas, but in the nineteenth century the family emphasis could still maintain the secular-religious balance. Irving and Dickens may have played down the religious Christmas, yet they still regarded it as an integral part of the day.

But, as all of us know, the twentieth century would expand the secular Christmas to new, larger dimensions, much but not all of it fueled by consumerism.

Yet, perhaps surprisingly, the religious Christmas would not just survive in a consumerist atmosphere but even flourish, and would do so in some unexpected ways.

CHAPTER SEVEN

The Feast of Christmas in the Modern World

Today many religious people lament what they consider the decline of the religious Christmas. Bumper stickers tell people to "Put 'Christ' Back in Christmas." Others prefer the phrase "Jesus is the Reason for the Season." Many identify a religious celebration as the "true" meaning of Christmas.

But these concerns are not warranted because, as I hope to show, the religious Christmas is alive and well but not in the traditional form. Furthermore, it has a bright future, in spite of consumerism. But before considering that future, let us first take a look at the current Christmas.

Some of the practices of previous ages continued. Poets continue to write religious Christmas poetry; the Nobel Prize winner T. S. Eliot (1888–1965) wrote the magnificent "The Journey of the Magi," but in the age of HD television and the internet poets no longer command the attention they once did. (How many people can even name their country's poet laureate?) Composers continue to write religious carols, but, with a few exceptions, the modern ones have not gained much popularity. John Jacob Niles (1892–1980), an American folklorist, collected Appalachian carols, and in 1933 he published the beautiful "I Wonder as I Wander." In 1958 Katherine Davis worked with choir director Harry Simeone to produce the touching "Little Drummer Boy." Yet people still mostly prefer "Silent Night," "The First Noel," and other older carols. The best-liked secular Christmas song of the modern era has been Irving Berlin's "White Christmas," but it has not replaced the religious ones in popularity.

Christian writers and directors have produced films about Jesus' birth, including the recent and realistic *The Nativity Story* (2006), but the blockbuster Christmas movies, such as *Miracle on 34th Street* (1947), *White Christmas* (1954), and *Home Alone* (1990), have all dealt mostly with the modern secular Christmas.

Into the nineteenth century a prominent venue for Christmas values was the church sermon. Modern preachers like Martin Luther King Jr. (1929–68), Billy Graham (1918–), and Joel Osteen (1963–) have shown that it still has power, but few preachers have national reputations or audiences in the way that bishop Fulton Sheen (1895–1979) did in the 1950s. Many now serve in megachurches with gigantic movie screens for easy viewing by the congregation, a far cry from the days of Peter Canisius and Lancelot Andrewes. In an attempt to update, some religious groups have gone on television. They have faithful audiences but pitiful ratings; their "TV stars" are literally preaching to the choir.

In general, the former, familiar means of promoting the religious Christmas no longer work as they once did in reaching large numbers of people.

Although not fundamentally opposed to the religious Christmas, the traditional secular celebration has still had an occasional negative impact on the religious season. In the modern era the most obvious casualty is Advent.

Traditionally Advent had been a penitential season, parallel to Lent and requiring fasting. By the nineteenth century Advent led up to a feast day that had come to include a secular element and that extended for several days of celebrating, but Advent itself remained untouched. Some churches even kept the Advent fast into the twentieth century. But when the secular Christmas expanded forward to the day after Thanksgiving in the United States and to even earlier dates in Great Britain and Western Europe, a penitential season became unpopular and then almost impossible. People have to shop for presents; how can one be penitent when one is thinking how happy a particular present will make a loved one? Office parties abound; how can one be penitent when one is eating sweets and often drinking alcohol? People put up lights, trees, wreathes, and crèches, all symbols of Christmas, not Advent. They hear Christmas music almost everywhere. Christmas movies play in the theaters, and every television program has its Christmas programs, even police dramas (crooks in Santa outfits). Those hosting the family Christmas must plan the celebration, hardly a penitential act. The pre-Christmas "season" has simply overwhelmed Advent.

The only truly visible manifestations of Advent can be found in churches, which may not put up a crèche until Christmas Eve or will put one up without a statue of the infant Jesus. Churches also resolutely refrain from singing Christmas hymns during Advent, which, while liturgically correct, means that people hear some genuinely beautiful music ("O, Come All Ye Faithful," "Away in a Manger") in stores and at home, while the Advent music sung or played in church, with the exception of "O Come, O Come, Emmanuel," rarely matches up.

As for the actual celebration of Christmas, the modern era has not added new elements but has expanded existing ones, sometimes to extravagant lengths as we saw with the Christmas lights. In some cases, this expansion has made the season even more fun. As we saw, in the late Middle Ages royal courts had Christmas plays and concerts. Now we have the ballet "The Nutcracker," the opera "Amahl and the Night Visitors," stage performances of *A Christmas Carol*, *A Christmas Story*, and more. There are frequent concerts of classical music (Bach's *Christmas Cantata*, Corelli's *Christmas*

Concerto, and, of course, Handel's *Messiah*) and popular music, such as carols but also "A Rock Christmas," "A Country Christmas," and the like. To this we can add the previously mentioned films and televisions, the "theater" in different form. Many of these secular attractions are intended for families and thus enhance the family character of Christmas.

By contrast, consumerist expansion of Christmas, including advertising, has actually impinged not just upon the religious one but also upon some secular holidays. Since sewing and embroidery and other handmade gifts take a lot of time, manufacturers make Christmas gift packets available as early as June. Summer visitors to tourist areas find Christmas decorations available for purchase, and many tourist areas have Christmas stores, that is, stores selling Christmas items year round. Some major American retailers now put up Christmas decorations after Labor Day (first Monday in September). This approach puts some pressure on Halloween (October 31), but that holiday can withstand it because it is a major event for children and has become so commercialized that retailers continue to promote it, especially with increasingly expensive costumes.

The truly threatened holiday is Thanksgiving (fourth Thursday in November), which itself has no consumerist overtones, the main reason people love it so much. An essentially modest holiday, Thanksgiving causes people to pause and thank God for their blessings. But the consumerist Christmas now intrudes on this day. Thanksgiving Day parades, sponsored by retailers, finish up with Santa Claus, the symbol of gift giving and thus of gift purchasing, and they do so well before people sit down to dinner. Christmas made-for-television movies, replete with Christmas gift advertisements, now appear before Thanksgiving. Worst of all, the day after Thanksgiving, the semiofficial American day to initiate Christmas shopping, has further challenged the holiday.

Stores used to open up at 9:00 a.m. on the Friday after, but then they began to open at 6:00 a.m., then 4:00 a.m., then 3:00 a.m., and, by 2010, some opened at midnight. Since people want places near the front of the line to get the supposedly fabulous bargains, they arrive outside the store several hours before the deadline. This means that to make a midnight opening, people must be at the store hours before then, which in turn means that they must leave their homes and families during the evening of Thanksgiving Day. Does anyone doubt that some retailers will open their stores at 11:00 p.m. on Thanksgiving itself (if that has not already happened someplace)? The traditional secular Christmas did not impinge on Thanksgiving, but the consumerist one has.

Aiding consumerism have been remarkable advances and innovations in advertising. The nineteenth century also advertised, but then "advertise" meant ads in newspapers and magazines, nonintrusive objects that could easily be set aside. By the early twentieth century radio had joined the list of advertising venues; television came along in the 1950s. All these methods still work, but now they have been joined by the internet, an important source of advertising since virtually everyone relies upon a computer at work and at home. Obviously, there is nothing inherently wrong with advertising; you are probably reading this book because of an advertisement. The problem with Christmas advertising is its almost exclusive focus on gift giving. The endless message to which we are exposed is that Christmas is about gifts and that there is something wrong with your Christmas if you do not buy and get or give the right gift. Let me emphasize that I support the right of retailers to advertise, and, in a time of recession, I am glad for the boost that Christmas gives the economy. My concern is that, however inadvertently, the message of commercial advertising boils down to this: Christmas equals gifts. Literally, nothing could be further from the religious feast.

People could respond that all religious people have to do is ignore the advertising; after all, televisions have mute buttons, and since internet advertising goes on all year long, we have all learned to live with it. True to a point, but people would virtually have to shut their eyes and ears to avoid all the advertising. They simply cannot avoid the impact of the constant bombardment to buy, buy, and buy some more.

The impact advertising has on adults can be multiplied exponentially for children. As early as 1951 sociologists began to notice that even children in religious schools identified Christmas with Santa Claus rather than Christ (Barnett, 56). The advertising industry has always employed many psychologists, and in recent years retailers have fine-tuned their approaches to children. Why? Previously advertisers of children's products would target parents who would make the decisions about what to buy and who often moderated what their children were exposed to. Now, thanks to the internet and cable television, there are endless venues for advertisers to reach children directly, which lessens or at least challenges the role of parents, especially their ability to say No. Since advertisers naturally want children to identify Christmas solely with Santa and gifts, their approach can only weaken children's appreciation for the religious aspects of the feast.

Advertising does not advocate consuming, which we all do, but consume*rism*. Christmas provides the opportunity for us to show what good parents and siblings and spouses and friends we are by the amount we spend on gifts for others. The more we spend, the more we care.

This attitude and not the traditional secular celebration of Christmas is what really threatens the religious aspect of Christmas, so let us now turn to that.

As we noted, many religious leaders bemoan what they perceive as the declining religious nature of Christmas. They often lament further that this reflects the general decline of religion in the modern world. They may be right, but anyone familiar with church history knows that Christians have been saying that in every era. Too many Christians idealize and idolize the apostolic era, and after that they see nothing but decline. Like most forms of nostalgia, the religious kind has no basis in reality. Anyone venerating the apostolic age should read the apostle Paul's First Letter to the Corinthians. Paul tells of jealousy, bickering at liturgies, sexual immorality, and Christians dragging one another into law courts. And all this in a letter to people he refers to as "saints." One shudders to think what the sinners must have been like.

To this we can add the disputes among Jesus' disciples as to who was the greatest; the intra-Christian conflicts mentioned in the epistles of James, John, and Jude; and the accounts of persecution in the book of Revelation. No matter when we look in Christian history, we will always find the same group: sinners. So let us abandon the notion that our age is somehow worse than all that went before. Christians of all eras are the same sinful people trying to be better, failing, trying again, and always relying on God's help to do so. At least the retailers do not wish to throw us to the lions.

Like other eras of Christian history, ours has its strengths and weaknesses, and it also has new elements that we must understand. For example, attendance at services has been a standard measure of the churches' vitality, and that is certainly down for both Catholics and Protestants. But is churchgoing a reliable guide? To cite my own church, on polling forms, many people who do not attend mass still list themselves as Catholics. As a churchgoer myself and an employee of a religious institution, I have difficulty understanding how people can claim to be Catholic and then show up in the pew only at Christmas and Easter. On the other hand, anyone thinking religiosity requires institutional activity should reread Luke's parable of the Pharisee and the publican, in which Jesus considered the repentant publican more justified than the religiously observant Pharisee. Clearly, people like me must try to comprehend the more informal, less institutional attitude that many modern and younger believers take.

We should also apply that attitude toward the religious Christmas. It is taking on new forms, and we must try to understand them.

Here are some thoughts on how this might be done:

First, a primary fear of religious leaders is that the secular Christmas detracts from the religious one. This fear derives partially from the erroneous belief that Christmas was somehow an innocent religious feast from its inception until the nineteenth century when unscrupulous merchandisers turned it into a commercial madhouse. As we have seen, Christmas has always had a secular element. To be sure, Medieval peasants did not celebrate it the way modern democratic people do, but their Christmas still had a secular element. As we also saw, people on the American frontier managed to combine the secular and religious elements, and, generally, so do we. The traditional secular Christmas has never been an enemy of the religious Christmas. Furthermore, we know that the secular Christmas does not have to mean consumerism, a true opponent of gospel values.

Second, all churches preach the importance of charity. Obviously Christians should help the underprivileged at all times of the year, and yet nothing brings out our charitable nature like Christmas. But much Christmas charity derives from the secular celebration because people feel bad that the underprivileged, especially poor children, would not receive gifts or at least not very good ones. If my parish church is typical, Christians may buy toys for small children, games and sporting goods for older ones, and sensible gifts like clothing for children of all ages and for their parents. No matter how much this may embarrass some Christians, it is the secular holiday that has increased charitable giving, a very Christian value.

Third, churches teach the importance of family values, and many Christian leaders bemoan the current status of the family. They worry particularly about divorce and remarriage with blended families, which challenge the traditional notion of family as a once-married couple with children. As a married parent, I generally agree, but the traditional family should not be turned into the only definition of a true family.

Yes, divorce rates were lower in earlier ages, but that is partly because for a long time many Christian countries simply did not allow divorce. For instance, Ireland legalized it only in 1997. Also until recently, most marriages were arranged, usually to keep property in a family through the next generation. Marriage could involve love, but that was rarely the primary concern. And for too long many countries did not consider domestic abuse to be a crime. Many victimized women who would gladly have left their husbands simply could not do so. Low divorce rates simply do not prove that a particular past era had happier marriages.

Christians concerned about family values should reconsider the traditional secular Christmas. As framed by Washington Irving, it is a family celebration. It proclaims and supports family values: being together, remembering good times, recalling those who cannot be there for the celebration because they may have died or they live at a great distance, eating a family meal (a decreasing practice today), and making others happy by giving them gifts. When Irving wrote, he took such a family Christmas gathering for granted; we do not, and so we value it more highly. Yes, people eat and drink a lot, and yes, they exchange gifts, but anyone who has ever celebrated a family Christmas knows what the real gift is. Realistically, how are Christian family values better expressed than at what is usually designated the secular Christmas?

Fourth, this emphasis on family values can focus only on the traditional family but ignore people for whom such a family is an impossibility. I will contend here that one of the most important things Christians can do to revive the religious Christmas is to reach out in God's name to those who cannot celebrate the traditional family feast because they do not live in traditional families.

Church leaders may lament divorce, but the simple fact is that many marriages just do not work. Yes, some divorced people get back together again, but most do not, especially if one or both get married again and have children with the new spouse. Naturally this creates problems, which can be magnified at Christmas. One of my students told me that her husband and she spend Christmas Eve and Christmas Day driving around Chicago's suburbs visiting her father and his new family, then her mother and her new family, then her husband's father and his new family, and then her husband's mother and her new family.

Situations like that make the traditional family gathering impossible, not just logistically but also psychologically, since there may be tensions among the various ex-spouses. Nontraditional, perhaps, but these are still families, and Christian love demands that churches reach out to them. How wonderfully Christian of this young couple to let all four parents know that the couple still wants everyone to be family.

Christian outreach does not mean institutional acceptance of divorce but rather that churches welcome all people on the birthday of him who came to save us all.

Nontraditional "families" can also include people who simply never married and do not have immediate families; they can include families headed by single parents. Churches should also show care to couples who do not have children. A married friend who has no children told me once that it is very awkward to be childless on the archetypal children's holiday, and he finds no solace in church, where homilists often present families with children as normative. Churches must speak to everyone, even when this may be challenging.

Fifth, Christians can augment the religious side of Christmas with increased awareness of those who do not celebrate it. By 2009 only 78 percent of Americans identified themselves as Christian. The 22 percent of those who did not would include Jews, Muslims, adherents of Asian religions, ex-Christians, atheists, and agnostics. We should also remember that there are Christian groups, such as Jehovah's Witnesses, who do not celebrate the day. Christians must realize that the overwhelming presence of Christmas from the late fall onward puts a great deal of pressure on these people and especially on their children. Regrettably this is not an area in which Christians have taken the lead, but Jesus' parable of the workers in the vineyard shows that it is never too late to do the right thing and that parable of the Good Samaritan tells us that we must reach out to those of different traditions.

The twentieth century did witness a growing sensitivity on the part of Christians about the impact of Christmas on others. No Christian celebrates the day in order to make others feel bad; there is no villain here. But increasingly Christians have recognized the problems our day creates for others, and we have tried to understand their point of view.

Oddly enough, the most obvious religious impact of the secular Christmas has not been upon Christianity but upon Judaism. For generations Jews viewed Hanukkah as a minor religious feast that happened to occur in December. But with the relentless pressure of Christmas upon Jewish children, many Jewish parents, especially in America, helped Hanukkah to become a major feast, complete with cards, toys, and decorations. Many conservative Jews had strong reservations about this; many still do. But, as a Jewish friend of mine told me, Christians have no idea how difficult it is to be Jewish in December when Christmas appears to be everywhere. She added that a good part of the difficulty is that Christmas offers so much that is attractive, such as the lights, the trees, and the music. Who would want to miss out on such delightful experiences? Even Jewish adults can feel left out at Christmas.

Christians simply cannot allow their great feast to make Jesus' own people feel set apart. Perhaps greater awareness is called for; perhaps sometimes simple gestures will work. When my older daughter was a girl, her best friend was Jewish. At the advice of a rabbi in our university, I asked my daughter to invite her friend over to help us decorate our tree. The girl enjoyed herself immensely and got a chance to see Christmas as a family holiday and not just an excuse for gifts.

Muslims now make up a growing part of the populations of Great Britain and the United States, and Christmas creates problems for their children too. A Muslim colleague at the university gives accounts similar to that of my Jewish friend. An understanding approach to our Muslim friends and fellow-citizens represents another challenge for Christians.

I hope these foregoing five examples demonstrate that the religious Christmas still has a great role to play, not just when we attend church but also and especially when we demonstrate our values, our care for those who may face an unhappy Christmas, our love for all God's people at the time when the New Adam redeems us all.

And what of the future?

The secular Christmas will remain, and it should. As we have seen in this book and as many of us have experienced, there is no opposition between the secular and religious observances of Christmas. I suspect that my family's approach is typical. We go to midnight mass, and we open gifts on Christmas morning. We have a religious observance and a secular one, and we enjoy them both.

On the negative side, clearly consumerism will not go away. It might even continue to grow, but there could be checks upon it.

We have already discussed several ways in which Christians can demonstrate the importance of religious values, and perhaps we can show people that although gifts are good and pleasurable, they alone should not define Christmas.

One possibility for checking consumerism may be a silver lining from a very dark cloud, the great recession. Many families simply have less money to spend, and a consumerist approach is simply beyond their means. Perhaps a simpler Christmas with less expensive gifts and a greater emphasis on family togetherness will convince them that rampant spending does not define Christmas, an attitude they may keep when the awful economic drought has come to an end. Maybe the plight of these people might convince others to tone things down too.

A second force to counter consumerism is the environmental movement. Many environmentalists push for a green Christmas, one that does not challenge the creation with excessive amounts of waste. They point out that consumerism damages the environment because if having "things" is all that counts, then the Earth's resources can be ravaged to provide for our wants. Many environmentalists and those practicing ecological spirituality argue for a simpler Christmas by using natural materials and by giving natural gifts, such as plants or bird feeders. These groups join with advocates for the poor in urging people to buy fair-trade products and crafts made by native craftspeople in emerging nations.

Third and last is our constant great hope, the young. On our campus, students in Christian groups or even unaffiliated ones raise money for clothing and gifts for poor children, sell green gifts and fair-trade products, and help to organize campus liturgies. Yes, they plan to enjoy the secular Christmas, but they do not equate it with consumerism. Let us hope that they maintain those values as they move into positions of leadership in our society.

Let me close with a subversive suggestion.

I suggest that the retailers and advertisers also believe in the religious Christmas. That sounds like letting the consumerist fox into the Christian henhouse, but I think the suggestion has some merit.

Collections of Christmas stories abound, and many contain works by great authors such as O. Henry, Willa Cather, and Truman Capote. What is striking about these stories is that not one of them shows people achieving Christmas joy and happiness via a pile of gifts. Excluding mysteries (of which there are many), the stories focus on families at Christmas: happy families, unhappy families, families separated, and families united. They also focus on charitable acts and how people sacrifice to make others happy. Referring just to these three authors, O. Henry's "The Gift of the Magi" portrays people sacrificing what had been most important to them to make a spouse happy. Cather's "The Burglar's Christmas" recounts with an unusual family reunion and the triumph of maternal love over family problems. Capote's "A Christmas Memory" deals with how a sensitive boy is befriended by a slow-witted elderly woman and how they make a warm Christmas for themselves in spite of their mistreatment by an indifferent, harsh uncle who heads the household.

When we think of the commercial films that have lasted the longest, we find much the same. *Miracle on 34th Street* shows a young lawyer risking his career to help an elderly man who thinks he is Santa Claus and a cynical young girl who has never enjoyed Christmas. *White Christmas* shows two successful entertainers going well out of their way and spending a great deal of their money to help their retired World War II commander to save his inn. *Home Alone* is basically a comedy, but its central character, a young boy, finds being alone really is not the fun he thought it would be. He misses his family, even more so in the film's most touching scene when the boy helps his cranky, elderly neighbor become reconciled with his son.

I do not claim that viewers necessarily evaluate movies in this way; they probably just enjoy them. But when we examine the themes of so many films, we find that most have similar messages about family and helping people, especially the poor and the unhappy. I further suggest that retailers and advertisers recognize this. They might fill their commercials with consumerism, but they produce films and shows that rely upon the very Christmas values that oppose consumerism. This is a strange but real tribute to the endurance of those values.

Probably the best film in this category and the strongest proof of my theory is the little-known *The Christmas Wish*, a 1998 made-for-television film starring Debbie Reynolds and Neil Patrick Harris. Here is the plot:

A young man named Will (Harris) was raised by his maternal grandparents after a reckless driver killed his parents in an automobile accident. After his grandfather has died, his grandmother (Reynolds) goes through her husband's notes and discovers that every Christmas Eve he would bring gifts to a woman named Lillian. Puzzled and upset, she tells her grandson about this. Positive his grandfather was not unfaithful, Will determines to learn Lillian's identity. He eventually discovers that she is an invalid, confined for years to a hospital bed, and now near death. Will and his grandmother go to the hospital, where a nurse confirms that his grandfather had come to visit Lillian every Christmas and to bring her a gift. This upsets Will and his grandmother, but the nurse then goes on to tell them that Lillian has been horribly unhappy for years, constantly lamenting how she had caused an automobile accident that killed a young couple. Will and his grandmother realize that his grandfather had somehow found it in his heart not only to forgive the woman whose reckless driving had taken the lives of his daughter and son-in-law but also to try to alleviate her guilt-induced misery, at least in the Christmas season. This stunning revelation inspires Will and his grandmother to forgive Lillian in her dying moments.

I have never seen a Christmas production that brings home so well the Christian values of forgiveness and healing. And this in a film whose broadcast was routinely interspersed with commercials that advocated relentless buying.

Christians should stop worrying about Christmas. The true values of the feast may not be evident in the traditional ways, but they always manage to shine through, even in the most unlikely places.

This brief book has tried to survey the various aspects of the religious Christmas, the feast of Christmas, over the centuries. It has left out much, and for that I apologize, but full coverage of twenty centuries would be interminable and unreadable. The titles listed in the bibliography will guide you to some more in-depth works.

Have a Merry Christmas!

Bibliography

Andrewes, Lancelot. Selections from sermons. http://anglicanhistory
.org/lact/andrewes/v1/sermon15.html.

Augustine of Hippo. *Sermons for Christmas and Epiphany*. Translated
by Thomas Lawler. Ancient Christian Writers 15. Westminster, MD:
Newman Press, 1952.

Barnett, James A. *The American Christmas*. New York: Macmillan,
1954.

Baur, John. *Christmas on the American Frontier 1800–1900*. Caldwell,
ID: The Caxton Printers, Inc., 1961.

Bede the Venerable. *Homilies on the Gospels, Book One*. Translated by
Lawrence Martin and David Hurst, O.S.B. Kalamazoo, MI: Cister-
cian Publications, 1991.

Bellarmine, Robert. Selections from sermons. http://www.therealpresence
.org/archives/Saints/Saints_025.htm.

Boniface. *The Letters of Saint Boniface*. Translated by Ephraim Emerton.
New York: Octagon Books, 1973.

Bradley, Ian, ed. *The Penguin Book of Carols*. London: Penguin Books,
1999.

Browne, E. Martin, ed. *Religious Drama: Twenty-One Mystery and
Morality Plays*. New York: Meridian Books, 1958.

Canisius, Peter. Selections from sermons. http://www.therealpresence
.org/archives/Saints/Saints_030.htm.

Cecil, David, ed. *The Oxford Book of Christian Verse*. Oxford: Clarendon Press, 1941.

Declercq, Georges. *Anno Domini: The Origins of the Christian Era*.
Turnhout, Belgium: Brepols, 2000.

Dickens, Charles. *A Christmas Carol*. New York: Dover Publications,
Inc., 1991.

Durston, Chris. "Lord of Misrule: The Puritan War on Christmas 1642–60." *History Today* 12 (1985): 7–14.

Elliott, J. K., ed. *The Apocryphal Jesus*. New York: Oxford University Press, 1996.

Forbes, Bruce David. *Christmas: A Candid History*. Berkeley: University of California Press, 2007.

Golby, J. M., and A. W. Purdue. *The Making of the Modern Christmas*. Athens, GA: University of Georgia Press, 1986.

Gray, Douglas, ed. *A Selection of Religious Lyrics, Medieval and Tudor Series*. Oxford: Clarendon Press, 1975.

Gulevich, Tanya, ed. *Encyclopedia of Christmas*. Detroit: Omnigraphics, 2000.

Horsley, Richard, and James Tracy, eds. *Christmas Unwrapped: Consumerism, Christ, and Culture*. Harrisburg, PA: Trinity Press International, 2001.

Irving, Washington. *The Sketch Book*. New York: Oxford University Press, 1996.

Jacob of Voragine. *The Golden Legend: Readings on the Saints*. 2 vols. Translated by William Ryan. Princeton: Princeton University Press, 1993.

James, Francis, and Miriam Hill, eds. *Joy to the World: Two Thousand Years of Christmas*. Dublin: Four Courts Press, 2000.

Kelly, Joseph. *The Origins of Christmas*. Collegeville, MN: Liturgical Press, 2004.

Kennedy, Charles, ed. *Early English Christian Poetry*. London: Hollis & Carter, 1952.

Keyte, Hugh, and Andrew Parrott, eds. *The New Oxford Book of Carols*. New York: Oxford University Press, 1992.

Luther, Martin. Selections from sermons. http://www.orlutheran.com/html/mlserms.html.

McKibben, Bill. *Hundred Dollar Holiday: The Case for a More Joyful Christmas*. New York: Simon and Schuster, 1998.

Miles, Clement. *Christmas Customs and Traditions*. New York: Dover Publications, 1976. (First published in London in 1912; this edition is a reprint.)

Nissenbaum, Stephen. *The Battle for Christmas*. New York: Alfred A. Knopf, 1996.

Nixon, Virginia. *Mary's Mother: Saint Ann in Late Medieval Europe*. University Park: Pennsylvania State University Press, 2004.

Restad, Penne. *Christmas in America: A History*. New York: Oxford University Press, 1995.

Robinson, Jo, and Jean Coppock Staeheli. *Unplug the Christmas Machine: A Complete Guide to Putting Love and Joy Back into the Season*. Revised edition. New York: Quill/William Morrow, 1991.

Roll, Susan. *Toward the Origins of Christmas*. Kampen, Netherlands: Kok Pharos Publishing House, 1995.

Rose, Martial, ed. *The Wakefield Mystery Plays*. New York: W. W. Norton & Company, 1961.

Schmidt, Leigh Eric. *Consumer Rites: The Buying and Selling of American Holidays*. Princeton: Princeton University Press, 1995.

Stone, Brian, ed. *Medieval English Verse*. Baltimore: Penguin Books, 1964.

Talley, Thomas. *The Origins of the Liturgical Year*. Collegeville, MN: Liturgical Press, 1991.

Trexler, Richard. *The Journey of the Magi*. Princeton: Princeton University Press, 1997.

Walsh, Joseph. *Were They Wise Men or Kings?* Louisville: Westminster John Knox Press, 2001.

Weiser, Francis X. *The Christmas Book*. Detroit: Omnigraphics, 1990. (Reprint of 1952 edition.)